A Fine Line

For Betsy —
Who does so much.
Thank you for your
uplifting + generous soul.
Eileen Walton

A Fine Line

In Pursuit of a Normal Life

a memoir

Eileen Walton

authorHOUSE®

AuthorHouse™
1663 Liberty Drive
Bloomington, IN 47403
www.authorhouse.com
Phone: 1-800-839-8640

*Many of the names of the people in this book, and certain identifying
details, have been changed to ensure privacy.*

First published by AuthorHouse   10/12/2010

ISBN: 978-1-4520-6844-2 (e)
ISBN: 978-1-4520-6843-5 (sc)

Library of Congress Control Number: 2010912574

Printed in the United States of America

This book is printed on acid-free paper.

For Megan and David

Contents

Author's Note

Quotes on the pages facing each
chapter come from my journals.

Sanity must hide in plain sight—
it's so hard to see.

Chapter 1

How It Started

What was my name, the police sergeant wanted to know. I wasn't sure. Should I tell him the name that everyone had always called me? Or did he want me to make up a new one—a new name that would prove to him that I could tell what was really going on. That I knew that there were wise and enlightened beings in the world, and that I was ready to be one of them.

I couldn't decide what to say. The old name or a new one? And if I had to choose a new name, what would it be? I would only get one chance to get it right. If I missed, I wouldn't be included in that golden circle of beings.

Before I could think of what to say, he was on to his next question. I stood staring up at him. I had to look up, because his desk was built on a platform, like a judge's. The sergeant's platform, though, was a cheap wood, painted white. As I looked up, he seemed very far away, tough and burly in his blue uniform. There were a few other policemen scattered around, but they weren't talking to me.

The sergeant kept asking me questions. I was wary of verbal traps and hidden meanings. I didn't know how to answer him. The questions were too difficult. Where did I live? Was there someone I wanted to call? Did I have a boyfriend? Did I want to call him? The sergeant wanted me to answer. The other policemen seemed to be on his side. Several times it must have looked to them like I would speak, because one of them would start to reach for the phone. But nothing ever came of it.

Meanwhile, I had my own questions. Was the police sergeant really an enlightened being, someone I could speak to freely? What would happen if I said the wrong thing? Should I be talking to him at all?

Finally, he asked me a question for which there was only one possible response. Now, I could answer him. "Do you know where you were last night?" he asked me brusquely.

"In hell," I told him.

He stopped asking me questions then. He must have given some sort of signal, because the next thing I knew, two of his policemen took me out to their car. I went willingly, until I saw that they wanted me to ride in the back. The wire partition made the backseat seem a cage. I balked. The two policemen talked to each other and then asked me if I'd like to sit in the front. That was fine, and I was skinny enough so there was enough room for the three of us.

I didn't know where we were going, but I wasn't worried about it. We stopped first at a deli. One of the cops got out and came back with coffee for him and his partner. For me, he brought back a cup of tea and a pack of cigarettes. They were Winstons. I didn't think anything of it then, but I do now. The gift of it.

Our next stop was a local hospital. The policemen left me there with the emergency room staff, who wasted no time in giving me something that knocked me out. When I came to, I was tied to a bed. They had used one of those long stretchy bandages and wrapped it around my palm, and then around my wrist. They used the ends of the bandage to attach my wrists to the bedrails. They had spread my legs so they could tie my ankles the same way.

I knew they were going to rape me. Physically restrained, I couldn't move—couldn't run, couldn't fight. I had never known such fear. It hit me in my belly, then snaked down into my crotch and through my thighs.

I kept looking at the hospital clock on the wall. How long before it would start? Whenever someone came into the room, I would think it was starting. People came and went. I lay there. After a while, they knocked me out again.

When I woke up, I wasn't tied down anymore. I found myself in a ward surrounded by dull metal doors with little square, reinforced windows in them. The doors I tried were locked. One day I sneaked down to the doors at the end of the corridor, trying to escape. The corridor was dark, with a deep brown linoleum floor. I thought no one would see me. I reached the end of the corridor without being stopped. The area was empty, no offices for the staff or rooms for the inmates. No one was there. I could see a staircase through the little windows in the doors. They couldn't be locked. How else could you get up and down the stairs? I was pleased, but it was short-lived. Those metal doors wouldn't open. They were locked too. There would be no escape.

All the doors in my section were locked. At night I was locked into the room I shared with another woman. My roommate yelled and cursed at people who weren't there. Though shorter than I was, she was hefty. I knew I would be no match for her if she attacked me.

Although there were plenty of locks in our section of the hospital, there was one exception: the bathroom. The toilet stalls had no locks. They had no locks, because they had no doors. Just a row of stalls with no doors. Maybe they were under construction. I mean, you couldn't use the toilet without a door. I went to find one of the nurses to ask where I could find a regular bathroom. With a little amused smile, she told me that that was the only bathroom for patients, and I would have to use it. I could hardly comprehend what she was telling me. I just couldn't use the toilet without a door. Somebody could see.

A fellow patient improvised a solution. Amanda was a large woman. She stood with her back to me at the stall while I used the toilet. She was my door.

Amanda was not very bright. She was fat and round, and not very self-assured. But she was bright enough, and kindhearted enough, to come up with her idea. Afterward, we walked down the hall together holding hands, she beaming with pride, me feeling grateful beyond belief.

I hate to think about Amanda. I hate to think about that cop. Sometimes that happens when someone's been good to you, and you really needed it.

Meantime, I take my happiness as it comes.

Chapter 2

Just Before

At age twenty, I wasn't too adept at picking men who were good for me. Character wasn't nearly as important as good looks. I wanted excitement more than true affection. I fixated on Mark, a big, good-looking guy a year ahead of me in college. He was tall, dark hair to his shoulders, and brown eyes, very deep, very dark. Did I say tall? Did I say broad chest, strong arms?

He always had a cigarette in his mouth—Marlboros, naturally. Sometimes he tucked a pack into the rolled-up sleeve of his T-shirt— very cool. I saw him once in a tux. He looked easy in it, a sophisticated charmer.

Usually, he drank beer, but sometimes he drank Scotch. Hard liquor. How cool was that? He smoked marijuana, but rarely; he wasn't really into it. That was the one disappointing thing about him.

He wasn't just a college kid. He had had experience in the real world. He had been in the army; he'd served in Vietnam. That made him a few years older than the average college student. It also made him less naive, less callow. I liked that about him.

He didn't talk about the war much, and when he did I could understand why. It was a war of horror and brutality; it repulsed him. In our college cafeteria there was one table that belonged to the Vietnam vets. Whenever I sat there, they were never talking about the war either. But underneath the chatter I could feel the bond that made them different. They weren't necessarily more mature than the other students, but they were more knowing.

Mark would break my heart a few times before we were through, but that was life, wasn't it, all that angst? His friends had warned me away from him. He lied; he cheated; he used people. I suspected that even his tenderness was calculated. But I thought him the sexiest thing alive. That's what I got out of the relationship. He was sexy; that meant that I was too. He made me feel so "on the brink." I was being let in on a secret, about what life was really all about. What he got out of it, I suppose, was that I was yet another woman who could bolster his insatiable male ego.

Despite deceit on his part and a willing naiveté on mine, the relationship lasted three years. I met his family; he met my parents. We had pet names for each other. He would occasionally take me to the movies. We went to see *Barefoot in the Park*. He loved it; he laughed out loud.

We spent a lot of time with his friends. One of them told me that he'd like to go out with me. I couldn't keep seeing Mark, though. Rich didn't share. He was monogamous. Rich didn't just want his woman to be monogamous, he was that way himself. That was just the way he liked it. That, in itself, would have been a nice change. Rich was also good-looking and tall. I liked tall. He had blond hair that flopped down just over his ears. He was thinner than Mark, but surprisingly strong. He was smart. He had a good sense of humor, but he just didn't send off the sparks that Mark did. Rich wasn't as flamboyant, not as center stage. I was a fool and passed up the chance for a gentler, kinder relationship. Looking back, it was a pivotal moment. Things would have been different for me. *I* would have been different. It hurts my head to think about it. In all likelihood, it would have been just as superficial though. Nobody was making any deep commitments back then.

Mark had been married once. It was disastrous and didn't last long. Maybe that contributed to his being so callous with women. He hated the idea of marriage; any man who wanted a wife was an idiot. As to a woman who wanted a husband, well, that was par for the (predatory) course. He was proud to tell me once that he had talked a friend of his out of marrying. His friend had phoned and actually asked Mark to talk him out of it, because he was dangerously close to getting hooked. Mark went through the list—it gets boring, you can't make any decisions on your own, she'll turn into a nag eventually, and every other argument he could think of. He stayed on the phone for over an hour. He didn't give up until his friend was finally convinced.

"Thanks," breathed his friend, and hung up. Mark was quite pleased with himself. He had saved a man from matrimony. As much as I idolized him, I was appalled that he would interfere in someone's possible happiness.

I was appalled by him another time too. It happened when my mother died, from a grindingly slow and painful cancer. I was devastated. I turned to Mark with my sorrow. He was sorry for my trouble, but he couldn't possibly be with me at the wake or the funeral, because he couldn't bear to be around dead people. He had seen too much death when he was in Vietnam. He said he'd be thinking about me. What good was that, I asked him.

What shocked me most, hurt me most, what shattered me, was that there was no offer to meet with me during those days. We could have met outside the funeral parlor away from where all the threatening dead people were. There was no offer—not even for a coffee shop visit, a cup of tea. My mother had died. He couldn't be with me for that? What could he be with me for? Anything? I knew the answer. Absolutely nothing, nothing that mattered.

I stayed at my father's apartment in Manhattan until the funeral. When that was over, I went home to Long Island to the apartment I shared with three other friends. We had met in college, and decided to take a chance on staying friends while living together. We were dissimilar enough so that we didn't get in one another's way, and similar enough to make the whole thing work.

Shortly after I got home from the funeral, I remember sitting outside on the steps one night with my roommate Elysia. She and I understood each other. We could talk for hours and not say the same thing twice. I felt she accepted me for myself. I talked about Mark. "I feel like I'm in a thousand pieces," I told her.

I stopped seeing Mark. Life went by. I moved to Manhattan, but I still thought about him. Of how woman-of-the-world he made me feel. I was such a fool. Even youth doesn't excuse it.

Somehow, even two years after we had broken up, I found out that he was tending bar at a place on Long Island. It seemed like a really good idea to just go out there and see him, surprise him. What a great idea. What made it such a spectacular idea was my newly found insight. I realized that the intervening two years had been a charade. He had loved me all that time. It was just a test. I realized that he'd never gone out with other women. That was just a test too. I finally saw what was really happening below the surface. Now that I knew, now that I saw all that—I could be with him. We'd be reunited, and we'd never part again.

I made the trip; I found the place. He was there, behind the bar. I must have started to get a little melodramatic. I know I made a scene of some sort. The bouncer took me in his arms and threw me out of the place. I walked down the block to a vacant lot and cried. I wailed. I shouted Mark's name and sobbed. A police cruiser came by. I instantly sobered. I didn't want any trouble with them. When they asked me what was the matter, I said I had had a fight with my boyfriend. They probably told me to take it easy or whatever cops say to defuse situations. Whatever they said, I agreed to do it.

They went away. I stayed there and began sobbing again. A couple passed me on the sidewalk, turning their heads to take in the spectacle, whispering to each other.

The bar closed up for the night. I didn't see Mark leave. I spent that night looking for him, looking for where he lived. I crossed through many backyards. I tried to lift up the doors to the basements. I was successful in one case and wandered through the house, calling his name over and over. A man came out of one of the rooms with two large black unfriendly dogs who were barking and showing a lot of teeth. "There's no Mark here," he shouted at me.

By now it was daylight. I ran outside trying to find my car. I didn't own a car, but I thought that one had been provided to me like a little gift from God. I tried all the handles of the cars, especially the blue ones. That was my color. It must have been a bizarre sight. The cops came and brought me to the police station, where the sergeant pummeled me with questions. All those confusing questions about my name, where I lived, did I want to phone someone, did I have a boyfriend, and finally, did I know where I had been the night before. The sergeant wanted to help me, I think. But that was impossible.

When the truth gets distorted, it's easy
to believe that there was no truth at all.

Chapter 3

The Dayroom

I can't remember everything that happened then. Both my mental state and the drugs that I was taking impaired my memory. My recollections are sketchy at best. I do know that after the cops abandoned me in the emergency room, I was transferred to a mental hospital, the one with no doors on the toilets and locked doors everywhere else. I remember screaming in my room at the hospital in the middle of the night, crying that I didn't know what was real and what wasn't. A nurse came in and gave me a shot of something that knocked me out.

At the hospital, we had limited freedom within the confines of the locked doors. The dayroom was our place, where we could meet and socialize. The room had Formica-topped tables, blue-green plastic chairs, and a short bookcase. *The Good News* was one of the books there. It was the New Testament, written in very modern English. I would pick it up once in a while, but always put it down before too long. It was hard to understand.

I had a friend. Joan was the only black female patient I ever saw there. She always sat alone at a small table against the far wall. She had just a medium build, but her muscles were hard, especially her arms. She looked as if she could take care of herself in a fight. Her eyes were usually stony, but then she could look at me with a certain light in them from way beneath, as if she were inviting me to fall into her eyes toward that light. She scared the other patients. She looked tough. She looked as if she belonged to a gang on the outside. I was never street smart or street tough. I had never had a physical fight in my life, not even as a kid. I should have been afraid of her, like all the rest of the inmates. I should have left her alone, as they did. But I wasn't afraid of her, and I didn't leave her alone. She liked me. I liked her right back.

Whenever I came into the dayroom, she yelled across the room to me in her loud voice, "Hey! Eileen!" "Hey! Joan!" I yelled back, just as loud. Then I'd go sit at her table. She had powerful energy. As I sat across from her, I could feel it bumping up against my own, taking over some of my space. We talked in short sentences and many silences. I always left her without a good-bye. I'd just get up and leave. No offense meant; none taken. I knew that she would understand that I had my reasons.

I made other friends there. One of them showed me pictures of her family. I would stare at each picture suspiciously, looking for something wrong with it. I was supposed to do that. I was supposed to find the thing that turned the innocuous picture into something that was threatening.

I saw a picture of her two children. The photographer's finger had covered part of the lens, and the finger came out in the picture. I pointed it out to my friend. That was wrong. It meant that the picture was unsafe, that I had almost been tricked into believing that it was just a picture of two happy kids. It wasn't. There was a foreign element in the picture; in this case it was a phallic symbol, which made it even more threatening. The picture was a trap. It scared me; all the pictures scared me; there was something wrong with each of them. The woman tried to reassure me with each picture. She was really a nice woman. I didn't believe her though. I knew that each picture was a trap, even if she couldn't see it, or said she didn't. Many ordinary-looking things were dangerous. I knew that much.

One day a doctor came to our dayroom, looking very busy and a little excited. He had some papers in his hands, and he went from one table to another talking to some of the women. He came over to me and told me that I could get transferred to a better hospital, a much nicer one. All I had to do was to sign my name.

I wasn't about to let him trick me. Who knew what he really had up his sleeve? I wasn't signing anything. Some of my friends tried to convince me that it was all right. They said that it would be better in the new place. The woman with the photographs told me that she had signed up to go there, and so had the others. I should do it too. I was suspicious of this supposedly good thing, this new hospital that no one had ever even seen. My friends believed this doctor, but I wasn't so sure that he was going to do what he said. He might be acting friendly just to get us locked up somewhere that was even worse than where we were now.

The doctor came over to me again. He put the paper in front of me and tried to talk me into signing it. I had already signed a confession, I told him. That's how I had gotten into this hospital. "Did you read it before you signed it?" he asked. No, I hadn't. "Then it's not a good confession. You're a lawyer. You ought to know that." I wasn't actually a lawyer, just a law student, but I had already learned about confessions. He was right. It wasn't a good confession. So I signed the paper he put in front of me.

Things slide, collide, mesh—who knows why.

Chapter 4

The Next Place

The next hospital was enormous—big social areas, extensive grounds, and many buildings, some like little cottages, some, like the one I was in, more institutional.

The doctor hadn't lied. The next place was better. We weren't locked into our rooms at bedtime. We could stay up at night and socialize. When we couldn't sleep, the women would gather around a long table, talking, smoking cigarettes, bumming them, giving them away.

We could go outside and walk around the grounds during the day. We could mingle with the other patients, even the men.

I noticed that one of the male patients kept following me. He had dark hair and a beard. He had a big stomach. He never said a word to me. He was quiet and brooding. He walked slowly and was big and heavyset, like a movable boulder. Wherever I went, he would be there, just staring at me.

One day, I was with a couple of the other patients when he showed up. One of the patients I was talking with was Jimmy. He was short and lean, and his movements were very quick. He talked fast too, for that matter. Jimmy always insisted that he was not a patient. No, he had jumped over the wall onto the hospital grounds to get out of a knife fight. We all believed him, of course.

I told Jimmy that the big man scared me. Jimmy spun around and yelled to him, "Hey, you! Stay away from her!" Magically, the man turned and walked away. He never bothered me again. It never occurred to me that Jimmy would say something to the man. Jimmy was just a little guy. The man was certainly twice his size. I wanted to learn how to stand up for myself like that. Meanwhile, I admired Jimmy for it.

Besides socializing with the other patients, I found some things to do on my own. There was a jigsaw puzzle I was working on, I remember. I loved jigsaw puzzles. I could lose myself in them and shut the world out. Unlike the real world, all the pieces fit together. They made a pretty picture. I could bring order out of chaos. As I was working on it, I saw a bug crawl out from under one of the pieces. I don't know for sure if the bug was real or not. I think it was. I screamed and brushed the puzzle to the side, scattering the pieces. I wonder if a member of the staff saw me, and dutifully wrote down in my chart that I got agitated working on jigsaw puzzles.

This place was far better than the last hospital I'd been in. Here, I was treated more like a patient than an inmate. I certainly had more freedom of movement. There must have been locked doors, but they were unobtrusive. I was free to walk around the grounds, seemingly at will. One night I got lost. The hospital grounds were vast, and the buildings all looked alike. It was late before I finally made it back to my own building. I remember asking the nurse on duty if I looked pretty. I was proud of my newly bought green satin top and white, pleated skirt. She agreed that I looked pretty, but she didn't sound enthusiastic about it. By then, I had been wearing the same clothes for days. I probably looked like a party decoration long after the celebration.

I liked having more freedom. Not only could we walk around without supervision, but we could make phone calls from one of the pay phones they had.

But I couldn't leave, and I knew it. The freedom went only so far; I was tied to someone's control with invisible, but very real, strings. It was still a mental hospital. I knew that I was being confined. I knew that I had a home, and that I was being kept from it.

No shoulds
Accept
Allow
Pray
Be on the lookout
Wait
Pounce

Chapter 5

My Apartment

I wanted to be back in New York City in my studio apartment, a fifth-floor walk-up on East 89th Street. I had no roommates, and I liked living alone. Although I had gotten along well with my former roommates, there were drawbacks to living with other people. Living alone, I didn't have to talk to anyone the minute I walked in the door. I didn't have to work my shower schedule around someone else's, or agree on what groceries to get. I didn't have to see eye-to-eye with another person on everything, from which mirror to buy to which record to play. I didn't want any more compromising. And I wanted to know that no one was looking over my shoulder as I explored my life.

Even for a studio it was a small place, but it could hold my bed, my dresser, a director's chair, and a small table. On the floor were a little black-and-white television, a stereo, and a Navajo rug (my pride and joy). One wall of the studio was exposed brick. So bohemian, I thought.

Living alone, I could listen to the music I liked whenever I wanted. I had the standards: Janis Joplin, Joan Baez, Cat Stevens. Back then, I could sing along to every song. I still remember at least half the lyrics to Janis's "A Woman Left Lonely" and all of "Bobby McGee." When I burned incense, I found the scent exotic. It conjured up an atmosphere of mystery; it made me feel intriguing and slightly foreign. I played a beginner's guitar, made assignations, and anticipated the objections of a late-night *Perry Mason*.

19

I was leaving my two-dimensional repressive Irish background behind, inch by inch.

Three of my friends lived right in the neighborhood—Fran, Manuel, and Angelo. Fran was an artist, in fact, they were all artists—a painter, a poet, and a drummer. I was the only one functioning in the straight world. I was the traditionalist, looking for fulfillment within the confines of the corporate structure. I loved being included in their group. They were artists. Maybe they hadn't yet made their mark, but they were artists and I was included.

Every week, Fran and I had Sunday Morning Breakfast. We always referred to it by its proper title. We'd get bagels and lox from the deli downstairs and set them out on the floor of the fake fireplace in my apartment. I'd fix tea, and we'd talk.

The four of us got together often, usually at Manuel's place. At some point during the night, someone would pick up the guitar. Angelo (the drummer) was by far the best player. He was also the best singer. His low and easy voice mesmerized me. So did his open, easy manner. His deep brown eyes did too. And he was tall.

The four of us didn't go out much, certainly not to the movies or to bars. None of us had much money. Just owning a television with good reception was quite a coup, not that we watched it often. Going to a coffee shop was a big deal. It was a bigger deal for me; I was the poorest in the group. Sometimes the three of them would go to a coffee shop for breakfast, and then call me up so I could join them for a cup of tea.

When we met at Manuel's, the four of us would spend hours talking, laughing a lot, and voicing our strong opinions. If we were lucky, Manuel would serve his hot potato salad.

Easy times were put on hold when I entered law school at age twenty-three. My schedule didn't allow much free time with friends. I had a full-time secretarial job, which I hated. I hated the work and I hated the status. There were some people lower on the corporate totem pole than I was, but only a few: the receptionist, the guys from the mailroom, and the fellow in charge of the stockroom.

Going to school at night meant a four-year commitment. But I'd be a lawyer afterward. It was worth it. It was worth going to school four nights a week. I took two buses in order to get home. Sometimes it was a long wait—longer, if it was cold. By the time I walked in the door, it was close to ten o'clock. I hadn't gotten dinner at the school's cafeteria because I didn't have the money. I used to just get a cup of tea, join my study group friends, and socialize before class. I'd wait until I got home to fix dinner.

I had to be very careful with my money, since I had so little. In my four years of school, I treated myself to a cab just once. Some cabbies like to talk; some don't. This one didn't; we were all business. It was May, a warm and evocative night. The smell of the evening, part spring, part summer, came through the open taxi windows. When I was a few blocks away from home, I decided to walk the rest of the way. I wanted to immerse myself in the sensual gift of this night. I asked the cabbie to pull over and let me out. He told me, "If you don't have the money, don't worry. I'll take you home." It was so kind, and unexpected, and gallant. Sometimes that memory comes back to me. I always like that it does.

Sometimes when I got back to my studio, I'd be hungry, but I'd feel too tired to cook. That's when I'd plop down on the bed, fully dressed, and go with the ten-minute rule. If I was still awake after ten minutes, then I was more hungry than tired. I'd make myself get up and eat. But if I fell asleep within ten minutes, then I'd lie there with all my clothes on and sleep through the night.

The demands of law school didn't end with nighttime classes. On Saturdays, my study group would meet for a few hours at my apartment. There was always studying to be done. I used every spare minute—reading on the bus, on my lunch hour at work, or at night while I was cooking. It was a schedule that was very stingy with free time. I looked forward to my summers.

Summer—a season in which I can stretch, when everything is easier.

Chapter 6

Summers

When my first year of law school was over, I felt as if I were on vacation, even with a full-time job. I was free of the class schedule, and the hassle of commuting from work to school, then school to home. I was free of the constant studying, and the worrying about it when I wasn't studying. I was free to enjoy the summer nights in my favorite city.

One night during that first summer, I was coming home from work and passed a little shop. It sold trinkets mostly, small brass objects, incense, but also a little jewelry, and some clothing. I saw a dress in the window. I stopped and looked at it for a while. It was a long black dress—down to the ankles, nipped at the waist. No embellishments.

I wanted that dress badly. It wasn't expensive, but I knew I'd have to work overtime in order to afford it. When I went to work the next day, I asked the manager of my department if there was some overtime available. He asked me why, and I told him. He chuckled and said he thought we could "make that happen." When I had the money, I went into the little shop and tried it on. The shopkeeper beamed at me. "It was made for you," he said. I believed him. It was true.

I brought it home. Before I let myself put it on, I showered. I washed my hair, and let it dry naturally, as I always did in the summer. I got into the dress, and put on strappy black sandals. I even put on some makeup. Then I sat down in the director's chair, because I didn't have anywhere to go. I almost didn't care, though, because I was so pleased with myself.

I lit a cigarette. Before I had finished it, Manuel called to invite me over to his place. Fran and Angelo were already there. Happily, I dashed down my four flights of stairs, and walked out into a warm, sunny, summer evening. On the way to Manuel's, I was blissfully aware of men's heads turning as I walked by.

The summer ended, and I entered my second year of law school. There were fewer students than in the first year. The teachers had already told us about the overall 25 to 30 percent dropout rate. We were beginning to see the evidence. Second year was just as demanding as the first, but I'd gotten through the first year and I was going to get through this one and the two after that.

I already knew I could keep up with the work and the schedule. I wasn't going to be one of the 25 to 30 percent who dropped out. In first year, everything was new, but I had weathered all that. I knew the routine and the school itself was now familiar to me. The drab, tan-colored walls of the corridors were still the same, as was the small, pathetic-looking cafeteria. The course books were different, but they were just as heavy. I knew where the professors' offices were, where the cavernous room was where we learned the law, where to find the library, with its familiar musty smell coming from shelves and shelves of books, and which shelves were likely to hold the books I needed for my research. In first year, when my heels click-clicked on the library floor, I may as well have been shouting into the silence, "Female! Female present!" Men's heads would snap up from their books to see the feminine creature whose footsteps were destroying their concentration. By the time I was in my last year, there were enough women in the school that the sound of clicking heels didn't elicit that response. We had become part of the landscape. It was a measure of our progress not to be noticed.

Academic life suited me well enough, but, like everybody else, I couldn't wait to get out and start my career. I wasn't near to starting a career yet, unlike some of the students who worked at law firms, or for judges, or for a not-for-profit organization, or for some political figure. At the time, I still had that secretarial job, which I still hated. I was still typing up someone else's thoughts, answering someone else's phone, getting someone else's coffee, helping someone else hang pictures on his wall, making someone else's copies, taking someone else's dictation, arranging someone else's meetings, making travel reservations for someone else.

But midway through second year, I got a break. I changed day jobs. My new job was as a paralegal at an advertising agency. I had my own office. I liked that. I shared a secretary, Sara, with another paralegal.

At the advertising agency I learned the difference between advertisements and commercials. Ads were in print; commercials were on radio or TV. My job was to be sure the advertising was accurate and truthful. I heard stories about the old days. One ad agency was photographing a hair color ad, but the color didn't come out right in the picture, so they used the competition's hair color and passed it off as their own. Soup bowls used to have stones put into the bottom of the bowl, to make the vegetables and the other solid ingredients rise to the surface so that the soup would look heartier. Those days were gone, and now agencies had legal departments to ensure truth in advertising. I loved my job, loved being on my own, making decisions, using my brains.

When I finished my second year of school, I celebrated by throwing a party. Most of the guests didn't know each other. I had invited a mix—friends, some people from work, some from school. Everyone got a kick out of having to sit on the floor. Especially if they were crammed in next to someone they had never met. Three of the guys could play and took turns handing my guitar around. We sang. We drank. We talked. At least one romance was sparked. We got high on the intimacy of a packed room.

I had plenty to celebrate. I had another beautiful summer to look forward to. I had made it halfway through law school. I had a good job, good friends, and, of course, I had my apartment.

My past—so difficult sometimes.

Chapter 7

Not So Fast

Insanity struck me that summer, midway through law school. The July Fourth weekend of 1973, to be exact. I was twenty-five years old. I had no warning. No one had suggested that I had been acting strangely. One day I was normal; the next I wasn't. It just happened, abruptly, harshly. I never saw it coming.

I don't know how my family learned that I was in the hospital. I do know that they were shocked and disturbed by it, and wanted to get me out of "there" as quickly as possible. When my father came to visit me at the hospital, he immediately began making arrangements to get me out. In order to be released, the hospital required that some conditions be met. One of them was that I had to have a doctor on the outside who would accept me as a patient. Complying with the hospital's requirements would take time.

I didn't understand about delays or requirements. I phoned my father to complain. I didn't like it there. I wanted to come home. It was taking a long time. When would I get out? He began to cry. "I'm trying, dear," he said. I didn't understand why he was crying. I was so sedated that displays of emotion were foreign to me. I thought the crying was a little strange, different, interesting, but it didn't affect me.

My aunt Muriel and my uncle Willie also came to visit. They were my mother's sister and brother. My aunt was appalled at my grooming. "Eileen, your hair," she kept saying. It lay against my head, greasy and limp. I hadn't washed it for days. I hadn't had a shower. I hadn't changed my clothes. I couldn't understand why she was so upset.

My uncle Willie was a limousine driver, and he had driven his black limo to the hospital when he came to visit me. I was going to go for a ride with him somewhere. I didn't know where. It was supposed to be a treat. I had always admired my uncle Willie. He was a gruff, tough man with plenty of heart. I liked him. Before we left for the ride, though, he began yelling at me for something I had said. I didn't understand why he was making such a fuss. I just stared at him, not answering him. He was only a few feet away from me, but it seemed as though he were at the end of some long tunnel. Now he was making a scene. There was no reason for it. I found the whole thing inexplicable.

I was experiencing everything through a cocoon of drugs and psychosis. Everything I did made sense to me, while my uncle's anger, my aunt's concern, and my father's tears, didn't. I was behaving normally; they were not. Their displays of emotion were at most curious to me. I didn't appreciate that their responses to me were fueled by their concern. I didn't appreciate, either, that their responses were intensified by the fact that they had been through this once before, with my mother.

In an unusual moment of closeness, my mother had talked to me about the nervous breakdown she had had when she was in her twenties. She had been in a mental hospital for nine months. "I had shock treatments," she said. I pictured her struggling, arms and legs fighting, her head rolling back and forth, that quiet voice screaming, fighting the staff who were determined to give her those treatments. I understand that they give general anesthesia now, but not back in her time. How did she get through those months? She was such a slender soul.

When she told me her story, it made me wish that I had been alive during that time. I wanted to hold her back then. I wanted to have shielded her with my body. I wanted to have loved her with a bond that would have been too strong for insanity.

When I had my own experience, my mother had been dead for two years. I knew I should be grateful that she had been spared seeing me that way. But I wasn't grateful. I wanted her to be there. She was the only one who would have understood me. She would have known what it was like—the texture, the taste, the feel. She would have known what it was like living in a nightmare from which you could not awake. You were already awake. She would have known these things. The tone of her voice would have told me that I could listen to her, trust her more than I could trust the other people. She would have known what it cost me to try to grasp reality with a mind that was so weakened. She would have recognized my suffering and my struggle. She would have embraced me.

*Why can't I just accept myself as
the vulnerable creature that I am?*

Chapter 8

The High-rise

Finally, all of the hospital's requirements were met, including finding a doctor for me. My father had found him. His name was Dr. Schein. At first, I thought his name was Shine, which I took to mean sunshine. That meant that he was anointed with a golden energy. That was a good omen, I thought.

I was discharged at last. I didn't have my sanity hat on yet, though. I still needed watching. I needed a safety net of family, friends and medical care. I couldn't be trusted to be on my own; it wasn't safe.

I had to give up my apartment. The landlord was very understanding about the circumstances, my father said, and didn't hold me to the lease. I went back to the apartment in order to clean it up for the next tenant. I emptied my closet, which was small and therefore not a big job. The fellows in my study group came to help me empty the rest of the place, taking away the big stuff, sweeping the floor, cleaning the bathroom. I had the job of cleaning out the refrigerator. Some smelly mold had accumulated in the freezer. Removing it was a disgusting job. I held my breath a lot. At last, I said a silent good-bye to the brick wall, and we left.

I moved in with my father, who also lived in New York. He had a two bedroom on the seventeenth floor of a doorman building on the East Side. The wall-to-wall carpeting in his apartment was done in a powder blue. The living room couch was deeply cushioned and came with a matching chair. The two end tables each had a gilded statue serving as the base of a lamp. There were two matching bookcases, and a cabinet with a built-in stereo. The stereo had a beautiful sound, but I didn't use it much.

When I first moved into my father's place, I was not adept at even the most ordinary conversation. Processing thoughts took a long time. To others I must have seemed a little dull. They didn't know about the efforts I was making to sift through possible traps. Then I'd think that I was wrong, and there weren't any traps. But why had this word been used and not that one? Why did it look as though this person's face were about to morph into someone else's? Did the entire conversation mean something different from what it seemed on the surface? My attempts at comprehending conversation were like my trying to run with a broken leg, only no one could see my effort.

I kept asking my father what had happened to me. Something was very different; that much was clear. "You had a nervous breakdown," he would tell me. I had a nervous breakdown? Me? I would stare at him, not quite taking it in. I had entered that world? My mind had broken? No, that was something that had happened to my mother, not to me. Having a nervous breakdown seemed so crushing, so serious. Had that really happened to me, I wondered. After thinking about it for a few days, I'd ask him again. The thought that I had experienced a nervous breakdown was so monumental. I had to be sure that that's what had happened to me. My father got testy answering the same question. At the time, I didn't understand why he was irritated with me.

I wasn't the only one with questions. My father and aunt both had questions for me about the onset of my illness. They held off asking me about it until I had become rational enough to understand what they were saying. When I was finally capable enough to comprehend them, the questions were waiting for me. How had it started, exactly? Why hadn't I called them? Had I taken mind-altering drugs? They assured me that it would be all right if I had taken drugs, that they would understand. I told them that the only drug I'd ever used was marijuana. They wanted to know more. What about other drugs, they asked, telling me that I didn't have to be afraid. They would understand.

My cousins, Uncle Willie's daughters, asked me too. I'm sure my father and aunt encouraged them to. They probably thought that I'd speak more freely to my cousins, who were close to my age.

I liked being around Patricia and Kathy. They were outgoing, and they each had a laugh that made you want to get to know them better. They had a touch of worldliness to them, which I envied, and they were each beautiful. Patricia had striking, black hair, and Kathy was the blonde. They were glamorous and exciting. I admired them both. I wanted to be like them.

They were slightly older than I was, and I looked up to them. Whenever they did something particularly nice for me, it made me feel very special. That these extraordinary creatures would even take notice of me, would let me into their world, was so exciting. That they were generous and good to me, that they liked and loved me, that we were related and I would have them forever in my life, that was even better.

When I was down on my luck one time, Patricia gave me twenty dollars, when she really didn't have it herself. When I hesitated to take it, she said, "If I don't give it away, Eileen, how am I going to get it back?" If I was going out on a date, Kathy would offer to do my hair or fix my makeup, and she was never short on advice.

I could talk to my cousins about boyfriends, girlfriends, parents, about anything. Their perceptions about people could be sharp and unexpected, and I usually left our conversations a little less naive than when we started.

I loved them for their warm and generous natures. I never once caught them measuring me against a standard of perfection, or even excellence.

But, like my father and aunt, they also said that it was all right to tell them about drugs, that they would understand. What nobody understood was that there was nothing to understand. I hadn't used hallucinatory drugs. Even with the invincibility of youth, I was afraid of drugs like LSD. I knew that those drugs could give you a bad trip. They took over your mind. I would have no control over what I was seeing, or even thinking. Who knows what I might hallucinate? I had never wanted to risk that.

It was clear enough what my family was after. They wanted something simple to explain my breakdown, something to explain my fall from grace.

I was so intelligent.

I was so pretty.

I was so talented.

I had so much to offer.

I had always been such a good girl.

"You were never a bit of trouble since the day you were born," as my father used to say. (After this episode, he never said it again.)

How could I have shattered so badly, they needed to know.

How indeed.

When I went to see my psychiatrist for the first time, Angelo came with me. We arrived with no problem. Then Dr. Schein opened the door to his inner office. I couldn't go any further than the threshold. The office scared me. He scared me. I couldn't go in. I just couldn't. In the end, Angelo came in with me. I sat at his feet, my back pressed against his legs.

I was propped up by tranquilizers and sleeping pills all that summer and into the fall. Even that wasn't enough to keep the terror at bay. I was in no shape to return to work, so I had to give up the paralegal job—the office, the secretary, the work.

I had been hopeful that, when September came, I could return to school. When September came, however, it was obvious that I wasn't ready. I wasn't knee-deep in psychosis, but I was shaky. My mind and my emotional framework were still weak, too weak to grapple with things like legal concepts. I tried very hard all summer to be ready. I wanted to reclaim at least a part of my life. But when the time came, I accepted the decision not to return to school. It was clearly my only alternative. Maybe next year.

All that summer, I had struggled to be free of the thoughts that gripped me:

Everyone can read my mind.

People are in disguise. The person I see in front of me is, in fact, another person in disguise. I have to be careful to frame my conversation so that it is suitable to both people, because the disguise might be a secret. I can always tell when there is a disguise.

Everyone can read my mind.

Television shows are all about me. They are being put on for my benefit. The plots, the situations, the dialogue, are indications of my character, my thoughts and feelings. The show might praise me or ridicule me. Anyone can watch it, and learn all about me.

Everyone can read my mind.

Songs are all about me—aimed at me, not anyone else. Like television, someone is orchestrating what I hear. If a song comes on that I like, that helps me cope with being afraid, then I know that the person in charge is pleased with me. If the song scares me, then I know that I have failed somehow. Anyone listening to the radio station knows it too.

Everyone can read my mind.

Everyone in the world is already enlightened, except me. Everyone is laughing at me because I'm not enlightened yet; in fact, I am pitifully far behind.

Everyone can read my mind.

I have had secret gurus in my life. There are people in the world, disguised as ordinary people, who are in fact wise, enlightened beings. I have been in touch with some of them. They are following my progress. They know how I am doing. They are judging me accordingly.

Everyone can read my mind. I have no secrets. I have no privacy. Anyone can read my thoughts—all of them, every thought I have ever had. I am mortified. There is nowhere to hide.

Balance, balance, balance

Chapter 9

Aftermath

I recovered slowly over the course of that summer and fall, a little more each day. To other people, I appeared to be recovering faster than I actually was. That was because I kept most of my strange thoughts to myself. I had found that other people didn't always react well to my thoughts. Sometimes, they became alarmed. Even so, I occasionally took the risk and expressed myself without censoring my opinions first.

I don't know why I bothered. The results were always the same. There would be a little hushed silence. Then I would see the air in front of my face become a series of successive, translucent, planes pulsing outward away from me. (The planes remind me of what happens when I save documents on Word. A series of cascading boxes pulse out toward the document. My planes were something like that.) When that happened, I knew that I had done something inappropriate. It was an uncomfortable and awkward moment. If I wasn't careful, my freedom could be compromised.

I was afraid of losing my freedom. I didn't have that much of it to begin with. There was no point in voicing my thoughts if they were only going to get me into trouble. I didn't need to prove myself, to insist on my point of view. I didn't need to make other people agree with me. Acting that way would only result in less freedom. It wasn't worth it. I always thought Galileo did the right thing by agreeing with the Church's opinion on the solar system so that he could stay alive. Saying he agreed with the Church didn't change his opinion, and it didn't alter the facts. That made perfect sense to me. I was no martyr either. So, for the most part, I kept my thoughts to myself. As a result, I appeared better than I was. The tranquilizers also helped by keeping me subdued.

As time passed, I got some house privileges. I could be left alone for longer and longer periods. I could go out with friends during the daytime. As I got better at this, I could go out at night, too. No big parties or anything, just tame stuff, but that was enough for me. I still wasn't "all there," still had some delusions wisping around, still needed to improve. I was getting better though, in tiny increments, tiny fragile increments, but I was getting better.

My friends were very understanding during this period. I still wonder how I would have behaved in their place. Crazy people had always scared me. (Could I have had some sort of premonition?) I don't think I would have been such a good friend. But they were. One of my study group friends, Jeff, had told me repeatedly that I could call him at any hour of the day or night. One night I did call him at two in the morning, frightened about something my father had done or said. Jeff was as good as his word. We talked until I was reassured, and then I was able to get to sleep.

Angelo was especially attentive. He had been my boyfriend before I had the breakdown. He was still there for me, visited with me, walked with me, played his guitar for me. We went to Central Park once to hear an afternoon concert. Bleachers had been set up. We were sitting high in the back. It was summer, and New York hot. I was thirsty. There was a puddle of dirty, leftover rainwater at the foot of the bleachers. I ran down and drank from the puddle. People around tittered. Angelo came rushing down to me. I think we left. The thought of it shames me now, more than anything else from that period. More than being expected to use the toilet without a door, more than not washing myself or changing my clothes for days, more than any of the bizarre things I did or said, that one still makes me shiver inside, as if I had done it yesterday.

I didn't do too many outlandish things, propped up as I was by Thorazine, a potent tranquilizer, and by the fact that I was getting a little less disoriented as the days passed. I could enjoy my friends; sometimes I could make them laugh. I was coming along. When we got together at night, someone would always walk me home, and see that I got into the apartment safely. If my father was asleep, I would, very responsibly, go into the kitchen, take my Thorazine, take my sleeping pills, and go to bed.

The Thorazine was housed in a big, dark, glass bottle. It was kept with my sleeping pills on the white countertop in my father's kitchen. So many pills in the morning; so many later on; so many at night. I would dutifully count them out and gulp them down. The Thorazine pills were gigantic; they were a little difficult to swallow.

One night, I came home from seeing Angelo and went into the kitchen, as usual. There, on the white counter, was nothing. No pills. I froze. No pills? What had happened to them? What would happen to me if I couldn't take them? Had I put the pills in a different place and now couldn't remember it? Should I wake up my father and ask him? Would my father think that I was regressing? Would some of my house privileges be cut?

I looked on the other counter in the small kitchen, on the dining-room table, in the bathroom, in the living room. Desperately, I looked in the same places all over again. Then I went back to the kitchen. I opened the cabinets. Inside one of them, there they were. Thank God. Thank you, God. I didn't have to wake my father. I didn't have to admit to being irresponsible, forgetful, careless, or more demented than I actually was. I was okay.

Why, though? Why had they been moved? The more I thought about it, the surer I got that I hadn't moved them. It *must* have been my father. I had to ask him about it, because I was afraid of it happening again. The next day, I told him that I had found the pills *inside* a cabinet. He readily admitted to having moved them. He assured me that he had done it for my protection. He had been afraid that I would come home and not take the right pills in the right amount. He had thought that I would wake him up when I got home because I couldn't find the pills. Then he could make sure I took the right amount. He wanted to be sure that I didn't do anything wrong. But I hadn't done anything wrong! Why did my pills have to be taken away from me? I was too timid to ask him.

I continued to go out with my friends, and always found the pills on the white counter. Where they belonged. Then it happened again. Angelo had left me at the apartment door, and when I went into the kitchen the pills weren't there. They weren't in the same cabinet that they were in the last time either. I found them in a different cabinet. This time I didn't say anything to my father. I wanted to hide how scared I was to be without my pills. I didn't want my vulnerability to show.

One night they weren't in the kitchen at all. They really weren't. I searched all over. I searched the same places twice, three times. I searched in the bathroom, the dining room, the living room, even my own room. I couldn't imagine where they were. I would have to ask my father. I opened the door to his room. I saw that the door to his closet was slightly ajar. On a hunch, I opened the door. There, on the shelf, were my pills.

I started to piece together the evidence. The only time my pills were hidden was when I went out with Angelo. If I went out with my girlfriends, the pills were on the counter. I never told my father that I noticed that. I didn't want to face his feelings about my going out with Angelo. Feelings that seemed possessive, controlling, and resentful. I just mentioned that I would really like the pills to stay on the counter; I was capable of taking them myself. I didn't need him to watch over me. My father finally agreed, but not without sulking. He was great at it. A stupor of silence, self-pitying stares in my direction, and a scrunched-up face, a guilt-inducing face, a face that telegraphed "See how you hurt me."

Being an adult and being crazy is full of contradictions. In some ways I can take care of myself, but obviously in some ways I can't. A good caregiver can treat you with respect even when you can't take care of yourself. That's an art. My doctor can do it. He makes it look easy.

When I could ride in the elevator in my father's apartment building by myself, I'd sometimes go down to Lillian's apartment on the third floor. Lillian had a warm, sunny disposition, with an excitable, and giving nature. She was more my father's friend than mine, but I liked her very much.

One night, I went by myself to her apartment. She had some of her friends over; they were watching the Watergate scandal unfold on television. They started discussing whether certain Watergate material should be made public. One of the men asked me what I thought.

At the time, I thought that everything on television was about me. I thought that they were actually discussing whether the public should have access to my diaries. Should my diaries be exposed, made available for anyone to see? I considered this question carefully; it meant a lot to me. Finally, I answered the man. I don't remember what I said to him, but he seemed to like the answer. In fact, my father later told me that the man had thought that my answer was astute. Astute. Why not?

I began to be so presentable, with the aid of my tranquilizers, that I could go out to a restaurant with my father. We were walking along the street on our way to dinner when I noticed some birds sitting along a telephone wire.

"Those birds frighten me," I said to my father.

"Don't look at them," he replied.

I tried not to, but every now and then I would look up to see if they were still there. Sometimes there were fewer of them. I thought that was a good sign.

We went to a local place for dinner. I knew I needed to act normal, quiet and polite. I worked hard at it. This was a special treat. I didn't want to mess up. Dinner went well. My father paid with a credit card. I thought that credit cards were a sign of enlightenment. The more you had, the more enlightened you were. When my father pulled out his credit card case, it was filled with cards. He must have had fourteen of them. I was overwhelmed to be with someone of such wisdom, someone so far up in the hierarchy.

The first signs of my progress were external. I could hold limited conversations. I could walk down the street without exhibiting any bizarre behavior; I could dress decently; I took showers; I could wash dishes.

Internally, however, I was lagging behind. I felt the terror of not knowing what was real, and an overwhelming feeling of humiliation. I didn't trust anyone. I couldn't trust myself. I didn't know what to hold on to. A tremendous force was raping my psyche. No one understood my struggle for survival.

As my bout with insanity receded in time, I could look back on it with a little more perspective. I thought about it a great deal. About the power of it, the strangeness of it, and, mostly, the tremendous violence of it. It had entered me, violated me, torn me into tiny, unrecognizable pieces. I felt a raw, hollow wound inside me.

I needed tenderness to help me heal. At the same time, I didn't want to treat myself any differently than I usually did. After all, it was over. I wasn't experiencing those feelings or those thoughts anymore. I didn't need any special treatment if it was over. That made sense.

As I often forgot, and as I was always sternly reminded, I couldn't bully my emotions into being what I would like them to be. I had to accept myself for who I was, and where I was on the reality scale. I did need to treat myself gently, with compassion. My mind needed to heal. My soul needed to heal.

I still need to remind myself that it's okay to be high-strung. I tell myself that some animals are made that way. Thoroughbred horses are like that, and no one condemns them for it. Maybe I am more easily jarred by loud music, the sight of litter, the suffering of people whom I can't help. Maybe I do need quieter moments, more beauty in my life, more solace than the average human being. Maybe my nerves are too—no, not "too," I'll say "very" instead—maybe my nerves are very sensitive. Maybe that's all right. Maybe I'm like those horses that need gentling down. Maybe I can accept that.

The insanity was the worst experience of my life; what came afterward was a close runner-up. Depression had a steel door that shut with a clang, trapping me in a windowless, cinder-block room. There was a timer on the lock. No matter what, that door wouldn't open for a six-month stretch of endlessly gray days and miserable nights.

After suffering from the misery of depression for those seemingly interminable months, it was finally over. I was once again able to hold a job. In March, I was a secretary again. Being a secretary meant being insignificant, even invisible. I couldn't help but compare this job to the paralegal job I'd had before. It made me hate being a secretary all the more. Where I worked, there was a clock on the outside of the building. If I got there a few minutes before nine o'clock, I would walk up and down the street rather than show up a minute before I had to.

At least the job brought in a steady income. I found an apartment. It was another studio, but not as small. The Navajo rug was once again in place.

When September finally came around, I went back to school. I had lost a full year. My former classmates were now a year ahead of me. I cringed with embarrassment whenever I saw any of them in the hallway. As for my new classmates, I didn't know a single person. I spent a lot of time in the ladies' room during the breaks.

There was only one person at school who didn't make me feel uncomfortable. Paul. He had never been in my classes (he was a year ahead), but I used to see him in the cafeteria sometimes. He had a slight build; there was something woodsy about him, and whenever I pictured him, he'd be wearing one of his plaid flannel shirts.

Paul used to joke a lot with one of my classmates, a guy who was painfully shy and equally nervous. Paul always got him to laugh. A real laugh. I happened to see Paul at school around the time that he graduated. I congratulated him.

"And congratulations to you," he said.

"For what?" I asked him.

"For coming back."

I was astonished. No one else had seen the courage beneath the fear. No one else, not even me.

While in my third year of law school, I went down to the basement of the school building where our placement officer had her office. She told me about a job as a law clerk that was available, but my resume had to be in that night. I didn't have one with me, and I was ready to walk away. But she sat me down at the typewriter and told me to write one on the spot. That's how I managed to leave that by-the-clock secretarial job, and become a law clerk for the Department of Justice. A federal agency—I had really arrived.

Another law clerk, David, started on the same day. He was a fine, decent, and good-looking man. We used to go to lunch together. When we were teamed up on a project, we managed to have fun. He could also infuriate me with his stubbornness, although I would call it determination when it suited me. His sometimes conservative viewpoints also irritated me. One day I called him myopic. He had to look it up in the dictionary.

He was quite taken with the fact that I had gotten the better of him by using a word he didn't know.

It took me a few months to realize that I was slowly, inevitably, falling in love. As we drifted from casual to serious in our relationship, I knew that sooner or later I would have to tell him about my episode with insanity. I was reluctant to tell him. I was ashamed, and he might stop seeing me once he knew.

For some time, I hinted that I had a dark secret in my past, but that was all I would say. I knew I couldn't avoid it forever, though. If he was going to love me, I had to know that he loved *me*, not some mirage. When I finally told him, I saw that I'd been worried for nothing. "Is that all?" he said. "I thought you were going to tell me that you were an ax murderer."

Physically, David was a big guy. He was over six feet tall, broad shouldered, and handsome in a quiet way. Light-colored hair, and sparkling blue eyes that hardened when he got angry.

David didn't shower me with flowers and presents, but he was thoughtful in other ways. To lighten up my drab apartment, which had a view of the apartment building next door, he refinished the floor. On a hot, close, New York summer day, David went to the store, rented the machine, and brought it back to my place. He went to work sanding the floor. I can see him now with that sander, sweating from the heat and exertion. Then he polyurethaned it. He did it twice, no cheating with just one coat. No man had ever done sustained, hard physical labor for me before. It was a gift that was better than dinner or flowers. I like a fine dinner, and I like flowers, but those could be bought. Besides, the floor lasted longer. When it was done, I would often look at it and smile a small, satisfied smile. David had done that. For me.

Things were coming together. I was happy. It was my final year at school. I had a substantive job, one that would look good on my resume, and David and I were together every day. When I finally graduated, I felt proud to have finished law school, even if it was a year late. I had survived the psychosis, not unaltered, but not totally defeated, either.

I thought I prayed all the time—maybe not.
How could I be like this if I was always praying.

Chapter 10

Again

After I finished law school, I started studying for the bar exam. I put in about eight hours a day. It felt like more because I couldn't stop thinking about legal problems while I was doing other things, like washing my hair, waiting on line at the supermarket, or even when David and I got together. Despite the pressure we each felt to study all day, we made time for each other in the evenings and on the weekends. Although our time together was technically time off from studying, we'd find ourselves asking each other some legal questions, or discussing things like the Rule against Perpetuities, or "the fruit of the poisonous tree" doctrine.

The booklets from the bar review course, lying on my kitchen table, were color coded, a different color for each subject. They were good study aids. Most things I was already familiar with, but I was surprised to discover how many technicalities had still to be mastered. In law school, I had felt anxious when I was studying. If I was studying torts, I'd feel anxious because I wasn't studying contracts, or something else equally pressing. I was only studying one subject at a time; it meant that I was letting all the other subjects slide. I knew that I was being absurd, but that didn't stop me from worrying.

Studying for the bar exam, I felt the same way. If I was studying that red-covered contracts book, my eyes would shift over to that yellow cover of criminal law. The green-covered book, the white, the gray, they all screamed at me, demanding my attention. My stomach would get queasy.

I couldn't do them all at the same time. I knew that in my head, but my stomach had a mind of its own.

I felt encouraged by the fact that I was studying at my red kitchen table. Three years before, I had scavenged it from the street, brought it home, and painted it red. I was very proud of this resourcefulness. It made me feel competent. That's how I wanted to feel for the bar exam.

My internship at the Department of Justice had ended around the time that I graduated from law school. On the positive side, being unemployed helped me prepare for the bar by giving me time to study. On the negative side, it also meant that I had to subsist on unemployment insurance. But it was summer, the easiest season in which to be poor. Dave and I walked around the city, went to museums, usually the Met, and often to Central Park. I also liked going to the department stores and using the perfume testers. I could treat myself by wearing a scent I couldn't afford, and I didn't have to pay anything.

I knew that my lack of funds would be temporary. I had good prospects. Soon I'd be enjoying the career that I'd worked so hard for. Study hard, pass the bar, get a good job. That was my mantra. I was happy to have a future to look forward to, and David to share it with. I would have a career and money soon, and I had love now. Everything was coming together.

But before I could take the bar exam, my mind deteriorated. I became entangled in engulfing fears, delusions, and assaults on my sanity that felt as though they came straight from the devil. In short, I became psychotic again. It was incredible that it could happen again. How could it happen again?

I had suffered so much the first time. Wasn't that enough?

Why wasn't it enough?

Being psychotic that first time had been the worst experience of my life. The worst experience that I could imagine. Now I had to go through it again? It wasn't possible. I had already paid my dues. I couldn't go through it again. It wasn't fair; it didn't make sense; no one could expect me to do this again. It was too much. I didn't deserve it. I couldn't take it.

There was something else. If it could happen twice, then it could happen again, and again. There was no limit to the number of times my psyche would be assaulted. How could I stand it? I had been naive to believe that the illness would be just in my past. It was going to haunt me for the rest of my life. It would change me, and transform my life. The prospect was hideous.

During the second episode, I had all of the same symptoms that I had had in the first. As part of the disorientation I felt, ordinary objects were scary and seemed out of place. When I looked through a magazine, the models were looking back at me, staring demonically as if they were living on the page. Over the years, I learned to use the models' eyes as a barometer for how I was doing. If I could look at a model's face without seeing her eyes boring into mine, then the worst of the episode was over.

As before, I thought people were in disguise, pretending to be who they were not. They were making fun of me; it was a big joke and I was the butt. I knew everyone else was more enlightened than I was. They were laughing at me, because I was so far behind them. Scariest of all was thinking that all my thoughts were exposed. Anyone could know my innermost feelings, not just then, but going back in time. Anytime at all.

There was the same distortion of television and radio. People could read all my thoughts, past or present. I was suspicious of everyone, believing that they wanted to ensnare me in some nefarious plot, or to dupe me into doing something that they could ridicule. I couldn't decide for myself what was real and what wasn't. I couldn't trust my thoughts. How could I possibly know if I could trust someone else?

Trusting came very slowly—only a little bit at a time—but it did come. I began to place my confidence in two people, just tentatively—my therapist and David. My therapist brought his professional acumen, David brought his love, and both brought an exceptional combination of character and concern. Slow as it was, my recovery was made just a little quicker by the presence of these two men in my life.

For most of the episode, it was dangerous for me to be alone. David and my father took turns being with me. David showed great equanimity when I was psychotic. It didn't shake him up. At the time, I wasn't aware enough to appreciate his attitude, but I learned to appreciate it over time. As I progressed slowly toward normalcy, he remained unperturbed and patient. He never pushed me into doing something if I felt uncomfortable about it.

If I wanted to go out for a walk, we went. We walked at my pace, very slowly. If I felt up to getting a cup of tea at the coffee shop, we could do that. If going out scared me, then we stayed home. If I wanted to help him with the crossword puzzle, we worked on it together. One time he was amazed that I knew that one class of angels was called "seraphim." I was amazed that he didn't know it, because I thought that he was Jesus Christ. During these times, David's two bywords were "We can do anything you want" and "We don't have to do anything."

He hadn't been thrown by the illness when I first told him about it, and seeing it firsthand didn't faze him either. He treated it like he would a physical disease. He was concerned, solicitous, and caring, but not scared by it, not appalled. His lack of fear helped me be just a little calmer. I didn't have to try to hide my fears from him. My fears didn't scare him. I didn't have to pretend to be better than I was. I had enough to deal with as it was. During those recovery times, trying to appear better than I was wasn't easy, and it was quite stressful. David believed things would work out. That helped me believe it too.

During this second episode, the intensity of the psychosis was about the same as the first time. The depression that followed recovery, however, was worse. This wasn't the walking-wounded kind of depression. This was the pull-up-the-covers-stay-in-bed-all-day kind.

If I had to put it in physical terms, an ordinary bad day would be like a stomachache. If I had a stomachache, I'd feel uncomfortable, my stomach would be uneasy, and I might sip some ginger ale to help with the queasiness. If I had an ordinary bad day, I'd feel blue, have a little less energy, maybe worry about something. An ordinary bad day is heaven compared to depression.

If an ordinary bad day is like a stomachache, then depression is like food poisoning. When I've had food poisoning, it doesn't just concentrate in my stomach; it affects other areas of the body as well. In fact, there isn't any place in the body that feels good—skin, organs, limbs, everything suffers from it. Sometimes I wish I could just go ahead and die.

In a similar way, everything I am suffers when I'm depressed. It's not just my mind that's affected; it's my emotional life; it's my physical life. Everything around me is gray, and so am I. I'm wrapped in a gray blanket. I'm sick throughout my being. I'm exhausted by the task of staying alive when nothing matters because life is meaningless. I'm exhausted by constantly making the decision that I will stay alive. I'm exhausted by the determination not to sleep all day. (I'm not always successful at that.) I'm exhausted by the pressing weight of that gray blanket. Nothing can make me smile, let alone laugh. I'm tired. I just want to sleep.

The only thing I have the energy to do is to roll into a ball and wish I were dead. When depression comes, about the only thing that gives me relief is sleep. It prevents me from feeling the sickness that is drowning my body, my mind, and my soul.

In this second depression, I slept all day; except for one half hour when I'd wake up to watch *Happy Days* on TV. Somehow, the show soothed me. It helped to know that everything would turn out all right, that the good guys would never get beat up, that the friends would stay friends forever, and that the family was there, providing a safe structure. I'd wake up each morning at 11:00, watch the show, and then go back to sleep promptly at 11:30.

I always went right back to sleep as soon as the show ended. I would sleep for a couple of hours and then open my eyes. I'd feel fleetingly grateful for the knowledge that I could close my eyes again and fall back asleep. So I'd do that—go back to sleep again. Left to myself, I would be in bed close to twenty-four hours a day. But I wasn't left to myself. I'd wake up around five o'clock, because David would be coming over soon. I was never happy to see him; I would rather have been back in bed. He came every night. I couldn't have been feeling any lower, or been worse company, but he still came every single night. David gave me pep talks, which was about as useful as offering a bone to a cat. I tried to humor him though. I knew he was trying hard. Did he know how hard I was trying? Did anyone?

The depression lasted ten months, my longest. I felt low, solitary, and vulnerable. Life meant nothing. After a couple of months, I got over the stage of sleeping so much, and could walk around. I slogged through each day. I wondered how other people managed. Nothing anyone did mattered. How did they go on? Would there ever be an end to this for me?

Getting healthy took a long time, but eventually I could feel myself getting better. I wasn't laughing yet, but I wasn't screaming the nightmare scream of an Edvard Munch painting, either. I could bear it. I could wait it out. I wouldn't kill myself.

In March, I had to take the bar exam. Taking the March bar would mean to other people that I had failed the first time. Why else would I take it in March? How could I get a job if I hadn't taken the bar on time? I was feeling overwhelmed, and worried because I was still living on unemployment insurance. The checks covered my rent, and kept me in hamburgers and tuna fish. Would I get a job before that source of income dried up?

What would I say on a job interview when they asked about my taking the March bar? What about when they asked me what I had been doing between graduation and the bar exam? In my head, I kept wrestling with imaginary interview scenarios. I couldn't come up with something adequate. I was too inexperienced to realize that projecting confidence was what would win that game, not the words I did or didn't say.

David, of course, *had* taken the bar in July. Official notification of the results would come by mail. However, the names of those who had passed were always printed first in *The New York Times*. At last, the list of names was to be published. David went to the newsstand that night and waited for the morning papers to be delivered. He hung around the newsstand along with a crowd of other attorneys-to-be. Once the *Times* arrived, the crowd jostled and grabbed for the papers, while the newsstand owner yelled out the page number of the results. David came back to the apartment, flushed with happiness. He had passed. I tried to be happy for him, but it was too high a hurdle.

He got a job soon after that. Again, I couldn't be happy for him. There wasn't a spot in my soul that was available to wish him happiness. All I had was that gray, nauseous feeling of depression. It permeated me. The nearest I could come was wishing that I did have that free spot, for his sake.

It's amazing that love can stay alive in the midst of so much frustration and unhappiness, but I must admit it does.

Chapter 11

Marriage

David helped calm my fears when I was in an episode, and encouraged me when I was depressed. But whenever I told him that I was grateful for his patience and support, he didn't like it. He complained that it made him sound like a Boy Scout. I looked it up. A Boy Scout is supposed to have traits like Loyalty, Helpfulness, Friendliness, Trustworthiness, Courtesy, and Kindness. Yeah, that's right.

Sitting next to David while he was watching baseball has always been very relaxing for me. At first, I didn't know much about the game, so I didn't get caught up in the excitement. The drone of the baseball announcers was just a soft buzz in the background, like bees in the summertime. Because I wasn't paying attention to the game, I was free to think my thoughts, or read a book, or just relax with a cup of tea.

With total lack of comprehension, I would hear things like: "And it's high and away"; "He's behind in the count"; "It's a called strike." Even the things I did understand didn't command my attention: "And two men left on," "And the score is now…"

Sometimes, I even napped in the living room while David was watching the game, I was that content. Then, one day as I was taking a nap, I was woken up by Dave saying loudly and excitedly, "God, what a pitch!" I went back to sleep, and the same thing happened again, and again. He was watching the Mets' Doc Gooden throw his fast ball. After being woken up like that a number of times, I finally asked Dave what made that pitch so great. So started my baseball education. Since that day, I've learned a bit about the sport. Now, I can tell you about tagging up, and why you should never slide into first base (unless you've already gotten to first base, and are on your way to second and have to come back).

"The boys of summer" they call the baseball players. From the beginning, I saw David that way too. Summer was his season. He didn't find the cold weather bracing, and the diminished sunlight was something he could never accept. He loved the sun; he loved being in Central Park with its lake and open spaces, enjoying the genius of Frederick Law Olmstead.

When I first knew David, he used to run the marathon early in November, and train for it for months ahead of time. A short training run would be six miles. As the marathon got closer, his longer runs could stretch up to twenty-two miles. I could never understand the fascination. It seemed like a lot of work and sweat to me.

When he was indoors, he read *The New York Times*, and remembered everything he read. He knew the background behind social issues and politics, and never seemed to forget anything, including where we had had dinner the year before. I called him "Answer Man."

One day David brought me home to meet his folks. "This is low key," he told me, maybe ten, twelve times as we drove out to Long Island. "This is low key." When we arrived, my in-laws-to-be did their best to put me at ease. They were warm and relaxed, and laughed easily. They made it as low key as these things get.

Three years after we had started dating, David finally proposed, and I said yes to the man I'd been waiting for. I was thirty when we got married, and it seemed a good way to start off the decade. We had the wedding reception in our one-bedroom apartment in Manhattan. The platters of food, the cake, and the champagne all came from local stores. I had told each of the storekeepers, "It's for my wedding." "It's for her wedding," they'd repeat happily to their coworkers. They all smiled and congratulated me. Small town New York.

I also rented tables, and white folding chairs, and gold-rimmed plates, glasses and flatware. I bought some irises and placed them in glasses on the tables. I didn't want a caterer. I didn't want the blasé energy of some waiter, who had seen it all before, to be a part of our celebration. I wanted only family and friends, people who weren't having thoughts of how-long-would-this-one-last dancing in their heads.

My cousin, Maureen, was my maid of honor. We had become friends over the past couple of years, after a lifetime of just being related. I was concerned that her sisters, Patricia and Kathy, might feel left out by my choice. After all, they were my cousins too. "Oh, no, Eileen," said Maureen, "as long as it's one of us."

Even the priest who witnessed the vows was in the family. It was very special to have my brother George officiate at my wedding. He had flown in from Seattle for the occasion. When he spoke in Church, he gave a little history about me. I heard later how David's side of the family appreciated learning a little something about David's bride.

I missed the presence of my brother Kevin, who couldn't come because of his military obligations. I missed hearing him say, "Eileen, here's the thing…," which was the introduction to so many of his opinions.

My brothers, both older than I was, taught me a lot as we were growing up. George tended to explain the philosophical matters, and Kevin the historical, though they did overlap. Sometimes their wit took the form of teasing when we were children, but only sometimes. I missed having Kevin at the wedding, but I was happy about everything else.

The apartment was small, and the guests mingled. There was one guest, however, who didn't move from his chosen spot. In the bedroom, where the mattress had been pushed up against the wall to make room, Uncle Willie held court. He told stories, and, with an Irish love of a good tale, he held a rapt audience. Uncle Willie usually didn't talk much. I knew that telling stories meant that he was happy—for me, and for the memory of his sister, my mother, whom he had loved so much.

My aunt Muriel, on the other hand, never sat still. She busied herself making adjustments to the food, socializing, smoking her cigarettes, and drinking champagne.

At the end of the night, as was typical in my family, the women cleaned up, but as the bride, I didn't have to do anything. Instead, I sat at our table, marveling at how easily women work together, and admiring the innate efficiency of the women in my family. They were intrinsically organized, like a gathering of ladybugs. My aunt announced that she wished there was more champagne because she just felt like having one last glass. We unearthed the last bottle, to her delight, and it was shared all around.

As the women cleaned up, the remaining men—Uncle Bill, Uncle Willie, Cousin Jack, and David—gathered around the radio to listen to the World Series. We had no television at the time. Without the benefit of visual effects, the men had to pay close attention to the announcers. They listened as the game unfolded play by play in their mind's eye. They hardly said a word to one another.

The wedding reception was, start to finish, exactly what I wanted. David and I began our married life, and had only occasional arguments. One year we were deciding where to go for vacation. I wanted to go to Arizona. It called to me, as I said at the time. I had never been there, and didn't know anyone else who had been there either, but I was determined to go. David, on the other hand, had several other vacation spots in mind. He wanted us to consider them all. "Can we discuss it?" he asked me, with an edge. "Yes, we can discuss it," I replied. "We can discuss what day of the week we're leaving, and what airline we're taking, but we're going to Arizona!"

We went in March, at a time when there had been an unusual amount of rainfall in the area. Everything bloomed. Even by the sides of the roads, there were wildflowers. The desert was a beautiful, haunted place. It was as mystical as I had imagined. We drove out to the desert one night under a not-quite full moon. We got out of the car and walked. I came across what felt like a sacred place. I knelt down and kissed the ground. The desert colors, the air, the cacti, the tiny flowers, the vastness, all filled my soul.

We also rode up to the Grand Canyon, which didn't have so many tourists at that time of year—a bonus for us. I loved how big it was. I loved that it was just as majestic and beautiful as people had said, that it had a presence. I loved that it was all those things, only more so.

On our way back to the hotel, we drove up a small mountain and delighted in seeing fir trees so close to the desert floor. At one point I took a nap in the car, only to wake up to David's voice saying "Eileen, wake up. It's snowing." Farther on in the midst of a cloud-filled sky, there was one opening in the clouds, with rays of sunshine pouring down to the ground.

One beautiful, moving, display from Mother Nature after another. David ended up loving the vacation almost as much as I did.

We were still newlyweds and loved being in each other's company. We went out to dinner and the movies, and we explored our city. I even enjoyed the mundane things, like making out grocery lists. That was how David got one of his nicknames. I had taped to the refrigerator a board for writing on (and wiping off). The board had four sticky little pads that adhered to the refrigerator. I was in the living room making out the grocery list, and I asked David to go to the kitchen and tell me what I had written on the board on the refrigerator. The next thing I knew, he was standing next to me with the board in his hand. He had just ripped it off and brought it in. "Igor" was all I could say before I laughed.

Two years after we got married, without warning and without any discernible cause, I started spiraling out of control. It was unfortunate timing, because David had gone away overnight.

I was convinced that I should get rid of all my possessions. I didn't touch David's things, but I threw out everything of mine that I could carry. I started throwing out my papers. I threw out the rental lease, my birth certificate, my identification, my journals, my poems, and my pictures. I threw out a picture of my mother that I had kept since I was a teenager. It had been taken when she was five years old. She was standing on a lawn, wearing a white dress, a bow in her naturally curly blond hair.

Later, when I got better, my family gave me some of their photographs so that I would have some of my own. One of the pictures of me bore a striking resemblance to the one of my mother—me at five years old, standing on my front lawn, a bow in my naturally curly blond hair. It always twists my heart a little when I look at it. We looked so alike. We looked like we shared a special bond. Of all the things I threw out that night, I try to think about my mother's photograph the least.

I took many trips to the incinerator room. I threw out my Navajo rug. It didn't fit in the compactor, so I left it there in a heap. Later, David talked to the apartment management about the possibility of getting the rug back, but it was gone. Someone must have seen it and taken it away, they said. I still think about the Navajo rug from time to time. I felt attached to it, in part because it seemed to hold out a promise for me of an intriguing life.

I threw out all the clothes in my closet. Only the empty wire hangers were left. When I had no more clothes to throw out, I thought I should throw out the clothes that I was wearing. I should go outside and walk down the street naked. I would show everyone how aware I was. I would show them that I knew that we were really supposed to be naked. That was the enlightened way to be. Everyone would take it as permission to stop the charade and walk naked also. I almost did it, but I listened instead to the tiniest of voices in my head that said no.

David came home the next morning. Instead of being my comfort, however, he terrified me. He wanted to kill me. I knew I had to get away from him somehow. I started talking about the hospital, and how I didn't want to go there. I thought that he would do just the opposite of what I wanted. If I kept saying that I didn't want to go to the hospital, then he would take me there just to spite me. I'd be safe from him there. It was the Brer Rabbit story.

I had seen the movie about Brer Rabbit when I was young, and the story stayed with me. Brer Rabbit had been captured and was threatened with a dire death. Brer Rabbit kept saying over and over again, "Do anything you want to me, only don't, don't throw me in the briar patch." Eventually his captor was convinced that the worst thing he could do to Brer Rabbit was to throw him into the briar patch, so he did. But Brer Rabbit had tricked him. The briar patch was where he'd grown up, and when he was thrown into it, he just scampered happily away.

The same theme appeared in *The Adventures of Tom Sawyer*, when Tom was painting the fence. To get what you want, just say you want the opposite. People will believe you. They'll do what you tell them *not* to do, whether that's being thrown into the briar patch, or getting your fence painted. But whatever my reasoning was, and whatever the precedents, David didn't go along with it. Instead, he kept reassuring me that I didn't have to go to the hospital!

I didn't know what to do. How could I get away from him? David had been staying right by my side—sitting next to me on the couch, and walking next to me as I paced the apartment. I was that frail and he was that concerned. I came up with a plan.

I paced the floor, holding a cigarette in one hand, an ashtray in the other. David stayed beside me. We walked back and forth in the living room. Suddenly, with a scream, I flung the ashtray and the cigarette on the floor. While he was picking them up, I ran into the bathroom and locked the door.

He tried to convince me to come out, but I knew better. He was persistent. I was clever. He was patient. I was adamant. I don't know how long I was in there. I do know that he finally convinced me to come out. Only a Boy Scout could have done that.

It was, as always, a time filled with many terrifying moments, and countless efforts to discern what was real. This time, as I came out of the mania, I expected the depression that followed. This time, it was the walking-wounded type. I could stay awake during the day. I could fix a cup of tea, pet the cat, and talk to other people, but all the while I was pushing a brick wall in front of me every inch of the way.

By the time this episode occurred, I was working as a lawyer. It was early in my career and I was eager to do well. I was concerned about the amount of time I took off as a result of my illness. Every episode required that I miss a number of weeks of work. When I returned to work after this episode, I was, of course, rational, but I was still depressed. One night, I had to iron a blouse to wear to work the next day. It was a brown silk blouse, with little brown buttons. Ironing meant that I had to set up the ironing board. I had to fill the iron with water, and reach down to plug it in. My cat had jumped up on the ironing board, and I had to pick her up and put her down on the floor. As I was putting her on the floor, she got heavier and heavier. For a moment, I thought that was significant, but didn't know what it meant. I had to put the blouse on the ironing board and press it, back and forth.

The brick wall I was pushing was very heavy.

As I was just starting to come out of the depression, I had enough energy to try it, just try it to see what it was like. I knew very well that it wouldn't be effective, unless I was in a tub of water. Still, I was fascinated by the process. I stood in our tiny Manhattan bathroom: standard white tile, gray rug, only so many square inches of space. I took the single-edged razor blade out of the medicine cabinet. With only a slight hesitation, I made a two-inch-long slit in my wrist. I saw the red blood in a thin line against my pale skin. In an instant, I went from being in a daze to having both feet on reality's ground. This wasn't something I wanted to do. I really didn't want to kill myself. That was just a fantasy. I wanted to live. The realization made me very happy. Hopeful, too. I was climbing out of the depression. I was in touch with what was real. I was in touch with my life.

I was so elated; I couldn't wait to share my discovery with David. Oddly, he didn't see it my way. He thought I had tried to kill myself, which was ridiculous, because you can't kill yourself that way. I don't know all the ins and outs of why you have to be in water, but everybody knows that you have to be. Why wasn't David happy for me? He called my doctor. Dr. Schein didn't seem to think this was the best thing I had ever done either. He suggested that David hold on to my sleeping pills, which he hid in his dresser. Why didn't anyone understand that this was a good thing? I had decided *not* to kill myself. I wasn't fantasizing anymore; I was back. Sometimes, nobody gets it.

People live in them [cultural/religious ideas].
No exit.

Chapter 12

Mom and Pop

Looking for a culprit for my bipolar condition, I turn easily to my mother. The threads of her shredded nerves have clearly been passed on to me. She had experienced her illness a little differently from me—she had had only one long episode, not multiple ones. Yet I know that sometimes she came closer than she would have liked to having another one, and it scared her. For weeks at a time, she would become tense and edgy. She'd complain, "I don't feel good, now!" or "I'm doing the best I can!" She was strident, her voice shrill, her clothing sloppy, her hair messy. It all contrasted sharply with her usual calm demeanor and gentle voice.

I can still hear her saying those things in her snappish way, but the remark for which she was most famous, good times or bad, was: "Don't upset your father." Having to tiptoe around my father's many moods put me on edge, and I chafed at the injustice of it. Looking back, I can see that in order for my mother to feel calm, she needed my father to be calm. She relied on him to at least partly shield her from the illness that had rocked her decades ago and was always threatening to return.

I remember standing in the living room with her one day when, unexpectedly, she turned to me. "Do you know why I never had another breakdown?" She paused. "My faith," my mother said definitively. I didn't believe her. How could religion save her from something that was medical, not metaphysical? I didn't contradict her though. If the thought gave her peace, she was entitled. I just wondered.

I wasn't all that clear as to what she meant. She didn't say. Did she mean, as I later discovered for myself, that if you clung to love, it would help you weather the episode? Or was it the religion she meant, with all its pomp and circumstance, all its structure? Nothing in my experience matched the structure of the Roman Catholic Church. You had a place within the structure. You knew what that place was. You knew what the rules were. If you followed them, your life would be in good order. They would ready you for the life to come. There were beliefs. You accepted them, and you didn't have to go exploring on your own for answers.

You could count on the Church's chain of authority. From the pope to the cardinal to the bishop to the priest. The pope was a spiritual leader, with authority and tradition to back him up. For one thing, he was infallible when he spoke "ex cathedra." Infallible. Unable to be questioned. Absolute. Totally right. One couldn't doubt him. At other times, when not exercising his privilege (and responsibility) of infallibility, he was a leader, and as such his teachings were followed. They were not questioned. Not when I was growing up.

My mother fit herself into that structure. She went to mass on Sundays, and frequently dropped in to church to "pay a visit" during the week. She belonged to the Rosary Society, a group of women who did good works.

She did good works on her own, too. There was an order of nuns, the Nursing Sisters of the Sick Poor. Each of the nuns was a nurse. They visited poor people who were sick, and ministered to them. They weren't allowed to accept anything except a glass of water from their patients. That rule was meant to save embarrassment on the part of the poor who might be unable to offer anything else. To get to their appointments, the nuns would have to walk or take buses. My mother used to drive them to their rounds. It made it easier on them, and perhaps they could squeeze in an extra patient along the way.

Our family was friendly with our parish priests, and they regularly visited us at home. One priest who was visiting our parish was a particular friend. He was a Maryknoll; he had been to distant countries to preach and minister. Like the Nursing Sisters, the Maryknolls saw a side of life that made them more down to earth, more appreciative of what life offered, more knowledgeable about what was really important. One day the visiting

Maryknoll priest phoned my mother out of the blue to say he'd like to pop down for a visit. He was only about fifteen minutes away. Trouble was, I had had a slumber party the night before and girlish paraphernalia was all over the house. Curlers, makeup, magazines, clothing—everything strewn all over. My mother got off the phone with the priest. "Girls, girls! Father Raymond is coming. We have to clean up. Hurry." Not only did we have to clean up, but girls in nightgowns had to get dressed. The rest of us swept things off the dining-room table and threw them into our capacious hall closet. Other things went upstairs. When Father Raymond finally arrived, the place looked like nothing had happened.

My mother enjoyed the company of priests. She loved to talk theology and philosophy with them. She loved being with people who shared her values, who believed in the same organization, who were on the same road to heaven.

Whatever the advantages to organized religion, one particular advantage to my mother was that her thinking about purpose and meaning was echoed by the Church. She found agreement on major moral issues. She knew what she had to do to lead a religiously satisfying life, and she did it, gladly. She belonged. She had faith, yes, and she also had structure. She had a God she could count on, and a way of life that was buttressed on all sides.

When my mother experienced her difficult times, it was obvious to all of us in the family, but I don't think an outsider would have guessed at it. She appeared to be simply a 1950s housewife (or homemaker as she preferred to say), involved in Church activities, a small social circle, and the care of three small children.

I was the youngest, so I got to stay home with her while my two brothers went off to kindergarten and first grade. Once every day, my mother would say to me, "It's time for your 'loving'." She'd pick me up and put me on her lap, and give me hugs and kisses. Then she'd put me down and not touch me for the rest of the day. I wanted to throw my arms around her during those lovings and hug her tight, but I wasn't brave enough. If I did that, she would know how much I wanted her closeness. What if she still only touched me during the lovings? I wouldn't have been able to bear it.

Growing up, my mother and I didn't share heart-to-heart talks. I was always censoring myself so that I didn't meet with her disapproval. But there was one thing that made me feel close to her: We were made out of the same stuff. Her nervous system was mine, her face and figure, her intelligence, were mine, her ailments, the way her mind worked, even her penchant for flattering hats. They were all mine.

That must have been what allowed me, sometimes, to know how she really felt, despite the face she presented to the world. As a child only eight years old, I suspected that she didn't love her mother. I asked her about it. I made sure to say: "I don't mean how Catholics are supposed to love everybody." What I meant was a mother-daughter love. I wanted to know. She sat down next to me on the couch. Without going into detail, she told me that she had had a difficult childhood, and that her mother had been less than caring. "I had a hard life," she said. No, she told me, she didn't love her mother.

I admired my mother for her altruism, her diplomacy, her generosity, the way she reached out to people. She once took our dog, Pudgy, to the vet, and saw a young girl there, maybe twelve years old, with her dog. When my mother was finished, she came outside and saw the girl huddled against the building, alone and shivering. Her dog had been put to sleep. Without a word my mother went over to her and held her, and the girl sobbed in my mother's arms.

I caught a glimpse of my mother one day in the kitchen. She was at the sink, washing the dishes, cloth in hand. I saw that she was "praying," "meditating," "in the Zen moment," whatever you want to call it. Everything about her was a prayer as she stood there. The washcloth was an instrument of prayer, the dish, her body, all instruments of prayer. Washing dishes—a prayer. Anything can be a prayer, I learned. Anything. I was awed by her.

As an adult, I was there when my maternal grandmother and my father were arguing in front of my mother. My mother sat, stone quiet, in the living room. "What's the matter, Mom?" I asked her. "Nothing," she said. "Nothing," she repeated, when I asked her again. Finally she confided, "It reminds me of when I was a child." I saw her then as a child, having to live with endless arguing and being helpless in the face of it.

I visited my mother every day while she was dying. Before she was bedridden, I saw her walking down the hallway to her room. I saw the effort it took her to do it. I watched as the cancer confined her to her bed, dependent on family and nurses. It was tough and raw and excruciating to watch her die. On one visit we weren't talking much, and then I said, "I love you, Mom." She answered, "I love you, too, but let's not tell anybody."

I still have no idea what she meant.

As for my bipolar condition, I really shouldn't let my father entirely off the hook. He often got depressed. His depressions were mild—not like mine—but still he had them. At night, he would sit in his favorite chair, a beer stein in his hand, staring blankly in front of him. He'd start sighing and saying, "Nobody loves me; nobody understands me." At other times, he'd get hyper. He was always anxious, always worrying about everything from his finances to whether we'd get to a restaurant on time. He would pace the floor, up and down, up and down, jangling the coins in his pocket. It was like he had a Worry-a-Day calendar that he used.

My father was a staunch Catholic and a traditionalist. In the 1960s the Catholic Church convened a council to modernize the Church, making changes in Church liturgy, and abandoning the Latin Mass. My father took that very hard. He came close to having a nervous breakdown. I remember him hollering on the phone for a solid hour, his face all red, arguing with the other person about "the changes in the Church." It wasn't just that one phone call either. He would get into a rage over the new liturgy with anyone who could withstand his tirades. Many conversations he had with people started innocently enough, but my brothers and I knew that somehow my father would find a way to steer the conversation to the topic of the Church. It was only a matter of time. His volatility lasted for over a year. Even later, when he was calmer, his opinion remained adamant; he never got over what he saw as betrayal by his Church.

Like most men of his era, he was something of a male chauvinist. He believed that a woman was useless unless she was pretty. This standard did not give points for character or talent. Eleanor Roosevelt was not admired in my house; she was ridiculed. After all, she had that warbly voice and unprepossessing face. According to my father's standard, all my worth was contingent on a value that age and circumstance would take away from me. To be fair, he did praise me for other traits, but I knew what was most important to him.

I remember the good things too. He loved talking with my brothers and me, always wanting to know what we were doing, what we thought. He liked to give us advice. He had favorite sayings, like: "First things first"; "Take it step by step"; and "Never compromise a principle. Compromise *within* a principle." And more whimsically: "If I can't wrap it up with wrapping paper and a bow, then I don't want to give the present."

My father worked as an administrative assistant to the chief executive officer of a growing pharmaceutical company. He worked hard at his job, and took a professional pride in doing it well. He admired professionalism in others, too. He admired the man who came to fix the boiler and left the area spotless.

He loved to counsel his nieces (my cousins), when they would inevitably phone with a problem they wanted to talk over with "Uncle Charlie."

He set a good example in caring for his elderly parents, in being devoutly religious, a loving husband, and an interested and devoted father. "Just do the best you can. No one can ask anything more of you than that," he used to tell my brothers and me. He joked that he wanted written on his tombstone: "He lived. He tried. He died." My brothers and I didn't do that, but it would have been apt.

The Catholic religion formed a basic part of both my parents' lives. They valued its ideals, its restrictions, and its orthodoxy. There was no thinking outside the box. When, at sixteen, I acquired a boyfriend, Freddy, my parents told me I could see him only once a month. Anything more would constitute a "near occasion of sin." That meant that seeing him more often would tempt me to sin. My religion required me to avoid temptations wherever possible. Allowing myself to be close to temptation, even if I never succumbed to it, was prohibited. My first experience with a boy was therefore strictly controlled. Despite my parents' restrictions, however, we got to see each other more often than once a month. We were inventive, and we had allies.

Freddy's mother was on our side. She would welcome me into her house so I could steal some time with her son. My friends also covered for us, making it possible for us to meet at the beach or the movies.

Freddy and I turned to subterfuge because arguing against my parents' restrictions was useless. They had too many institutions on their side. It was great training for me, though. I could go along with the mind-set, but, like Galileo, still believe my own beliefs. I could have been a spy.

Besides the overall moral issues, my father just didn't like Freddy. Needless to say, my mother followed suit. ("Don't upset your father.") When it came time for me to go to my senior prom, Freddy and I had been dating for two years. Naturally, I asked him to go with me.

My mother: "I don't know why you have to invite Freddy when you know it upsets your father." She told me how selfish I was, always doing what I wanted and not what was in the best interest of the family. She mentioned Tommy, a boy I had dated once, just once. Tommy had taken me to the Latin Quarter. The floor show had showgirls clad in practically nothing but feathers and pasties. I was supposed to make him my choice?

Despite my parents' opposition, I stood my ground and invited Freddy. The day of the prom, I dressed in my blue gown, fixed my hair, and applied my makeup (minimal). My mother came up to my room and told me again what a disappointment I was. Then she turned away and went downstairs in a thick silence that knifed my stomach into slivers.

My brother George came out of his room. He had heard every word, and the silence of the exit. I still needed help with the buttons on my long white evening gloves. They were impossible to do by myself, and besides, I was shaking. George did the honors in my mother's place.

Up to the last minute, I had hoped to hear a girlish "Have fun!" from my mother. She was in no mood for that, however. There were other things I would have liked to have heard from her. More than anything in the world, I would have loved to hear something like, "I love you for yourself, not because I need you to placate your father."

Do we ever get enough?

Chapter 13

Growing Up Normal

I grew up perfectly normal. Well, not perfectly. There was that time when I was fourteen. I lost all interest in school, friends, rock 'n' roll, longing for a boyfriend, everything. My energy was low. Everything was an effort. I didn't know what was happening to me. I was listless, and it was a struggle to hide how I was feeling from my family. I didn't want to have to answer their probing questions. I didn't want to talk about it, whatever it was. Besides, I didn't know what it was or how to talk about it.

I stumbled around in the grayness for three months. One day I went to take a nap in the back bedroom. My bedroom was in the middle of the house, and it was a little depressing. The view from my window spanned the alleyway and stopped at the side of the house next door. I used to open my window and lean out to look up at the sky when I was particularly lonesome for it.

Anyway, I went into my brothers' back bedroom. Where they were, I don't know. I took my nap. When I woke up, I looked out of their window and could see a blue sky with a few white clouds scattered about, and I knew that whatever it was, it was over. It left me that suddenly, as suddenly as it had come. Later, I learned what it was. It was my first depression.

Other than that, there were no signs of impending disaster. As a child, I enjoyed the company of my two older brothers, George and Kevin. I was two and a half years younger than Kevin and he was a year younger than George. With only a few years separating us, we were in one another's company a great deal. Kevin could draw very well, and he knew that I loved color-by-numbers. He would draw pictures, and then outline the areas for the different colors and number them for me.

The three of us used to watch television together: *Million Dollar Movie, Wonderama, The Millionaire,* and any type of mystery. When we were really young, we loved to watch *Winky Dink and You,* a children's show that always entertained us. First, we sent away for a kit that went with the show. Inside the kit there was a transparent plastic sheet that we put over the television screen. It clung there somehow, maybe from static electricity. There were different color crayons, which we divided up among the three of us. When the hero was in trouble and needed a bridge to cross over a chasm, for example, the television announcer would call out one of the colors of the crayons. Then he instructed the child who had that color to take the crayon and draw a line from one side to the other. The cartoon character would walk across on the line and be saved. By us!

As for parents, my mother was distant, my father was moody, but those things were not outrageous. They didn't fit into the Hansel-and-Gretel story. I don't think that anything but genetics made me bipolar, although my personality didn't help me to combat it. I was high-strung, mightily insecure and shy, and felt an overwhelming obligation to be perfect.

I grew up like any other kid. I had relatives who were favorites of mine, and relatives I could have lived without. I adored my grandfather. He came into the family by marrying my mother's mother. I was never fond of my grandmother, and often wondered what a man of such goodness saw in her. He died when I was six years old, but my memories of him are still vivid. He had a full head of white hair, and a mustache. He smoked a pipe and wore suspenders. He always seemed to be wearing a tie.

In the morning, before anyone in my house was awake, I'd run up the block to his house. "Your folks never take care of you," he'd say. "They never brush your hair." We'd sit on his porch together, and he would brush my hair. "Whose girl are you?" he would ask. I always said that I was his.

He was a fire captain in New York City, and I still have the picture of him in his uniform, with his cap on. He was a handsome man. To this day,

I'm particularly sensitive to fire exits. If I see that an exit is even partially blocked, I do something about it.

I told my aunt Muriel once that I was lucky that he died when I was so young. That way I didn't have to risk becoming disappointed in him, as I got older. "You would never have been disappointed," she said.

My aunt Muriel was also a favorite of mine. She doted on my brothers and me, bought us ice cream and clothing, snapped our photographs, took us to Broadway plays. At a time when all the women on our block were housewives, she wasn't. She was a *secretary*. She went into the city every day. She wore office clothes. She dyed her hair. She smoked. She was the epitome of sophistication.

Muriel could be a highly critical person, however. When I was a young adult, Muriel and I would often meet for lunch or dinner. Absolutely the first thing she did upon seeing me was to criticize something about me—my hair, my clothes, my skin, I was late, I was early, I looked tired, and so on. One night as my uncle was driving me back to my apartment, Muriel and I were sitting in the backseat, talking. Somehow, I got up the courage to broach the subject to her.

"The first thing you do when you see me is criticize me," I told her.

"There's a lot to criticize," she replied.

I didn't know what to say. When we reached my apartment, my uncle got out to walk me to the door. "Don't pay any attention to her," he said.

David used to argue with me that my uncle Bill wasn't really my uncle. He was only my uncle because he married my aunt Muriel. I had too many fond memories of him to consider him an "in-law." When my brothers and I were young, he babysat for us. We called him our companion, not a babysitter. We were much too grown up to be babysat. He loved to watch television with us, especially the mysteries.

One night, my uncle was driving me home from somewhere; we were listening to a detective story on the car radio. When we pulled into the driveway, the show wasn't quite over. I really wanted to hear the end, and I was disappointed that I was going to miss it. Instead of turning off the ignition and going inside, Bill left the car running until the show was over. It ended with "And that's it, Tom." Bill turned to me and said, "And that's it, Tom." We laughed and went into the house.

When my brothers and I grew older, we played poker with him. He took us bowling. He taught us how to keep score. He'd drive us anywhere. He loved to drive. When I was older still, and I visited Bill and Muriel after they moved to Saratoga, Bill would slip me a hundred-dollar bill, always saying, "Don't tell your aunt." My aunt would do the same, only she'd say, "How much did Bill give you?" He only stopped giving me money when I had a daughter of my own. When she was about ten years old, he started giving it to her.

David kept trying to drum it into my head that Bill really wasn't my uncle. I understood the concept; it just didn't apply, that's all. One day my uncle phoned, during one of my episodes, to talk to David about how I was doing. Bill told him, "I don't think of her so much as a niece, really. I think of her more as a daughter." That's when David stopped telling me that Bill wasn't "really" my uncle.

It's more than just intellect, guys.

Chapter 14

Catholic School

With my parents' strong religious beliefs, there was never any question about the type of school I'd attend. It was parochial school, of course. Kindergarten was rather sweet, but first grade was painful. There was a boy in our class named Artie. He was a nonstop talker. No matter how many

xxxxx ould not keep his mouth shut.

p to her desk. She took him by the She slowly led him toward the back and calmly, that when they got there, she ue out.

y and sob. When they were halfway to the back of nun said that she had to go back to her desk because she had rgotten to get a napkin "to catch the blood." By this time, Artie was hysterical. She took him with her up to her desk, got the napkin, and proceeded, once again, toward the back of the room. When she was halfway there, she stopped. She held Artie tightly by his hand, as he stood there, yelling and sobbing.

She asked the class if we thought she should cut out his tongue. Cries of "No, Sister! No, Sister!'" flew around the room. She told Artie that, only because his classmates had begged her not to do it, she would let him go this time.

We were so relieved, for Artie's sake. It had been a close call. The teacher not only had authority because she was our teacher, but she was also a nun. That gave her absolute authority. If she had wanted to cut Artie's tongue out, she had the power to do it.

After that, school life went on more or less uneventfully. Then in third or fourth grade, I raised my hand to ask the teacher a question. I was a good girl, smart and well behaved. Indulgently, she called on me.

We had been studying about Christ and the moneylenders, and how he had thrown them out of the temple, taking a whip to them, overturning tables, scattering coins. My question: "How come Jesus can get angry and we can't?"

The nun turned red. She yelled, "Because God can do whatever he wants to do. That's a very stupid question. Now sit down!" I sat down, crushed and humiliated, not knowing what I had done wrong. I know now what I had done wrong. I had asked a question to which she hadn't had an answer. An answer like, there's a difference between being angry at injustice, and angry from a sense of pique. I know now it wasn't a stupid question. (Can an honest question ever be stupid?)

I learned to keep my mouth shut. Questioning would get me nowhere. Exploring was taboo. High school was much the same, only more so, because as teenagers we had even more questions.

But I had other problems in high school. I was one of the smart kids. In fact, I had won a full scholarship to the school. My mother said she wasn't surprised; my father was a bit more excited.

Being smart was just one more teenaged embarrassment. It added to my feelings of awkwardness, like being a too-tall girl before the boys caught up. It was most awful in history class.

Mrs. Bruno was a good history teacher, and I liked her. She talked to us almost as equals, and she was passionate about civic duty. Local government was the most corrupt layer of government, she told us, simply because people would pay attention to their presidential candidates, but couldn't even name their alderman. If we didn't pay attention to our government, Mrs. Bruno would say, then we had ourselves to blame for the government we got. She talked about the League of Women Voters with respect, the work they did, their dedication to our democracy, and that we should make it a point to get to know more about them as we got older.

Every week Mrs. Bruno gave us a quiz. We wrote our answers on three by five index cards and handed them in. The following week Mrs. Bruno would hand them back. We had to go up to the front of the room and pick them up from her. She'd start with the highest score and work her way down. If a girl got 100 percent on the quiz, she would announce that. I always got the highest score. I always got 100 percent.

Every week when she called my name, I had to go up to the front of the room first. I would have to hear those words "one hundred." I was mortified to be the smart one. I didn't want to be different. I wanted to be like everybody else. I didn't even want to be admired. I just wanted to be accepted. I just wanted to fit in. After weeks of this, I realized there was something I could do about it. The next week I would deliberately get something wrong. It would be easy to do. I knew all the answers. Then I wouldn't have to go up first. Maybe I'd go up third. It didn't matter as long as I wasn't first. The next week, I waited to hear a name, any name, so long as it wasn't mine. And it wasn't. It was Barbara Miller.

Barbara had everything. She was rich, pretty, popular, and nice enough but not overly nice. Most of all, though, she was a member of The Crowd, a group of the most popular, glamorous girls at the school. It was so special that boys were members too, rich boys, boys going to prep school.

I expected that Barbara would feel some of the shame that I felt when she got her quiz back. But to my amazement, she obviously was pleased. And she had even gotten 100 percent! I could see by the expression on her face as she returned to her seat that she was proud of her achievement. That made me wonder. I knew I had to rethink things. Maybe being smart wasn't what made me different and awkward. Maybe it was something else.

I had my own friends, not enough to be called a "crowd," but a few. Annie lived not too far from me. We walked home partway many times from school, talking about our lives, what we wanted when we grew up, parents, boys, school, Annie's alcoholic stepfather. We talked about what bothered us, what we thought of our teachers. We didn't behave like silly teenagers. How many silly teenagers are there, really?

One of my other close friends, Mary Ann, had made it into The Crowd. I would have given anything to be a member of that group of sophisticated, cool, secure teenagers. I never said as much to Mary Ann, but she surprised me one day by saying, "I'm going to get you into The Crowd." I was thrilled at the mere possibility. She started a campaign, getting me invited to parties, getting me to hang around The Crowd girls in between classes.

I worked hard at it, but I was ill at ease, especially at the parties. The boys were worse to deal with than the girls. They were so smooth. They could dance well, dress well. They could flirt. As for the girls, I was always anxious around them. I wasn't sophisticated the way that they were. I had very little to say. I didn't belong. In my heart I knew it.

At school one day, we were taking a break in between classes. A couple of the girls from The Crowd were standing by the window, one of them sharpening her pencils. I got up from my seat and started to go over to them. Then I stopped. I didn't feel good when I was with them. I wasn't comfortable. I wasn't myself. I wasn't happy. What was I doing? I went instead to talk to Janice. She would never even be considered for The Crowd. She was overweight and had a plain face. She wasn't gaga over boys. She had other attributes that made her a good companion, however. I enjoyed her company, which was always kindly and genuine. So I stopped trying out for The Crowd. Game over.

In senior year, we had Sister Mary Anthony for math. Sister Mary Anthony said that since math was logical, everyone could understand it. If someone didn't understand it, that was because it hadn't been explained in the right way. Everyone was different. Maybe, as the teacher, she could reach a certain number of girls, but some would be left in the dark. That meant they needed someone else to explain it to them. Give it a different slant.

If some of us weren't able to do a homework problem, she would have a student who had solved the problem work it out on the blackboard, and answer questions, until everyone in the class "got it." I was impressed with Sister Anthony—that she wasn't threatened by her student's successfully explaining a problem that she hadn't been able to explain herself, at least to everyone's satisfaction.

She also enjoyed sparking discussions about mathematical concepts that had nothing to do with our studies. She wanted us to know that there was more out there, always more to learn. She was my favorite teacher.

The high school years weren't the rock-around-the-clock carefree beach party that I'd been led to expect from movies, magazines, television, songs, and my vivid imagination. We had problems more intense than what to wear or how to get that boy. Annie's alcoholic stepfather beat up her mother on a regular basis. Many times Annie and her mother would leave their apartment in their pajamas and walk the few blocks to Annie's aunt's house to get shelter. One day, Annie came to school with a black eye; the bruise was large and turning yellow and purple. I was standing behind her on line to go into class, and she turned to me and said, "My father hit me." She had been trying to stop him from hitting her mother, so he hit her instead.

My friend Janice worked after school to help her family. She worked at a department store, on her feet for four hours after school, four days a week. I distinctly remember being at our lunch table when one of the other girls said, "These can't be the best years of our lives." We all agreed.

During the summer of junior year, one of the nuns asked me, Annie, and two other friends if we would volunteer three days a week at a day care place for boys who were mentally challenged. The first day I went there I was a little apprehensive. Would this be more than I could handle? As soon as I opened the door to the building, the atmosphere of high-speed energy hit me. This was decidedly different from anything I had known before.

Some of the boys were as old as fourteen. I didn't usually work with the older ones. They were a little intimidating. I helped the younger boys to make shadow boxes, and we did other arts and crafts.

Billy was a big boy, about twelve or thirteen. He had gotten hold of a booklet full of math problems—simple addition and subtraction. He showed me a page he had completed, and I looked it over. "You got everything right," I told him. "Gee, Billy, you're smart." He went around the long table, showing every boy the page and saying "I'm smart. I'm smart." I realized that never in his entire life had anyone told him that he was smart. Maybe the work he did, and the thoughts he had, were smart for him. Maybe he tried hard, maybe he was an ordinary kid.

One day my friend Veronica came to school looking upset and shaky. She wouldn't say what was wrong. It was weeks later, as we were sitting at my kitchen table, that she told me that she had been raped. The doctor had given her some pills to calm her down, but she asked me to hold on to them for her while we were at school. I did it without question, but in hindsight I'm sure she didn't want to hold on to them for fear of taking too many.

One afternoon, Veronica came to class late. I was struck by how pale she was, and how troubled and anxious she looked. Without asking for an explanation, our teacher immediately yelled at her for not being on time. The nun could see only a disobedient student, and not the wounded and vulnerable girl standing before her.

It would be unfair to imagine that there was a total lack of, as they would say, "Christian charity" in my school, or that all the nuns' attitudes were strictly think-only-within-the-box. Just as unfair would be to say all the girls were snobs, snatching at a chance to make themselves superior even if it meant being cruel. Some of the girls were snobbish, true, but many were real-life and genuine, struggling to make sense of the lives they were given. Many of the teachers reached out to us, stimulated our intellects, invited us to do our best, and challenged us scholastically. The best of those teachers stand out even now, the ones I still want to emulate. But I remember most the moments when the opportunity for compassion arose and wasn't taken. I find it hard to forgive that. I do.

*Were the old times so good that
you'd like to go back?*

Chapter 15

College

When it was time to go to college, I knew that I was going to go to a Catholic college. I made sure that it was coed, but that didn't mean that it was without its restrictions. After a certain hour, the girls had to sign out of the dorm. We had curfew, of course, and we had lights out. Our RA would go around to check. After lights out, no phone calls were allowed on the one phone we shared on the floor. The college had a lake on the property, where the students could go and swim. When a girl walked down to the lake, she had to wear a raincoat over her bathing suit. The school didn't want the boys distracted by the sight of girls in bathing attire. The boys didn't have that rule. That's because the girls wouldn't be distracted by the sight of an attractive male in bathing attire. Right.

The college town was small. There were no traffic lights, just one stop sign. That was the whole town. There wasn't much to do, although once I went deer spotting with some friends. Being a city kid, I was fascinated by the sight of the deer, beautiful creatures who stood stock-still in the beam of our headlights. Spotting the deer over and over again, however, soon lessened its charm. It also gave me one less thing in common with the rural-based student body.

The school's policies were restrictive, designed as they were to keep the two sexes apart. It was easy for me to keep apart from the opposite sex; I was as shy as I had been in my all-girl high school. I missed my home town, too. One day I was crossing a campus road, right behind a truck.

I could smell its exhaust fumes. It made me nostalgic for the traffic of Manhattan. As for the school's academic life, that was fine, except that I hated my four hours of chemistry lab every Thursday (which was really not anybody's fault.)

I decided to transfer, this time to a non-Catholic college. My transcript was in good shape, except for chemistry. I needed a C in order to transfer those credits. I couldn't bear the thought of having to take them again in a new school. I think the professor took pity on me. My transcript was accepted! So in my sophomore year, I was attending college on Long Island.

I met people with different backgrounds, different religions, and some with no religion at all. I met people I could have conversations with, long into the night. I loved being around interesting people, all with a story to tell. One black woman I knew was engaged to a white man. I was bold enough to ask her how she felt about that. Wasn't it going to be really tough? She was a gentle person and had the inner strength that gentle people can have. Being interracial was going to be something of a problem, yes, but it was one she could deal with. I accepted that, and then asked her, "What about the hard part—that he's male?" We laughed. I wish I hadn't lost track of her.

I got involved in student politics. It took up more time than it was worth. Sometimes, without realizing it, I'd follow other people's dreams for me instead of my own. I'd always thought that there was something wrong with me because I had never been secretary of state, like Madeleine Albright. It only occurred to me later in life that I never really wanted to be Madeleine Albright. That was just a mistakenly borrowed dream, like student government.

At my new college, I took courses that expanded my outlook on life—the liberal arts courses, film, poetry, philosophy, English literature courses. They all opened me up. My drama teacher in particular was adept at pointing out things in art or life that I'd overlooked. When I'd been out of college for a few years, I saw a drama on television that riveted me. I dashed off a letter (before email days) to my former teacher, telling him that if it weren't for him, I wouldn't have seen so much in the drama or been able to appreciate it as much as I did. He wrote me back ("My dear

Eileen") thanking me. Like him, the letter was gracious and captured his generous spirit. Ever the teacher, he wrote me that the drama was one of a series, and that the last one was "devastating." I read the letter over often.

At college I didn't go to frat parties, I didn't drink; I just used marijuana occasionally. Actually, I did drink once. In the pursuit of discovering myself, I thought that getting drunk would be a good way to loosen some inhibitions, and get down closer to the core. So I went to a bar and drank several rum and cokes. The only other patron at the bar was a man approaching thirty, who was pontificating to me and the bartender. He told me that he could tell things about me. That was great! That was just what I wanted to know! "You're intelligent," he boomed.

"How do you know that?" I asked him. I was excited. I was going to get some reflections on my character from this personage.

"Because you don't get rattled when I talk to you!" was his answer. That's all he said about me. He went back to pontificating on another subject, spinning out stories and opinions that the bartender may or may not have heard before.

When I got back to the dorm, the women on my floor were shocked that I was drunk. "The judge is drunk!" I heard one of them say. The judge? Did I act like a judge around people? I didn't know that people viewed me that way.

I told my roommate, Nancy Mastrocancito, "I'm not drunk. I can say Mastrocancito."

"Yeah, but can you spell it?" she said.

"M-a-s-t-r-o-c-a-n-c-i-t-o," I proudly replied. That was the end of my coherent conversation for the night.

College was where I met Mark, who made me feel so grown up and worldly wise. We took many trips in his small convertible back and forth from his apartment to school. In the winter, Mark and I would drive around the school parking lot, looking for ice patches. He'd make the car twirl on the ice. I loved the freedom and risk of the turns, and I loved how competent he was at maneuvering his car.

At college I met the women who would become my roommates, and my friends. My friendship with Elysia even survived a coast-to-coast separation of many years.

I was happy at college. I was beginning to be a little bit wise. I had my life ahead of me, with no major obstacles. They were not the best years of my life, but they were good years. I didn't wait until I was older to look back and appreciate those times. I knew enough to appreciate them while I was experiencing them. I knew that I was lucky. I just didn't know how much.

The emperor has no clothes.

Chapter 16

The Church

We weren't just Roman Catholic, but *Irish* Roman Catholic. The religion was burned into our bones. All the Church's teachings, policies, rules, outlooks, manners, and regulations were echoed strongly in our home. Some of that was good. I was taught that there was purpose and meaning to my life, that I was unique and had a special place on this earth. I was taught that there were guiding principles to be followed, ethics to be adhered to. I was taught that all people were children of God and were to be treated accordingly.

This last point was something at which my mother excelled. For instance, she hired Jack as a handyman. He was a big, rough-looking older man, who wore dirty clothes and had a peculiar odor about him. We always referred to him as "Jack the Handyman," as if "Handyman" were his last name. I don't think I ever knew his real name.

Knowing that he could use the money, my mother would find jobs that she could give him to do. At lunchtime, she would always say, "Would you like a sandwich, Jack?"

"That's a good idea, Mrs. Sullivan," he'd always reply. He would say that again to an offer of another half a sandwich, another cup of coffee. Sometimes his odor forced my mother to leave the kitchen and busy herself in the dining room in order to get a breath of air.

My mother found comfort within the spiritual teachings of the Church, and also in its structure. The Church gave her a context within which to live, and helped her to weather the mental storms that threatened her from time to time. I felt an inclination to view life in some sort of spiritual way, as my mother certainly did, but eventually it would not be in the context of the Church.

I found its taboo on sexual intimacy chilling. Sex was prohibited except within marriage, and then only if I didn't practice birth control. Sex was touted as a blessing within the proper framework, and profane otherwise. It all seemed arbitrary to me.

In my twenties, I discovered D. H. Lawrence, and felt that he understood what I couldn't articulate. Later, I would alter my opinion of his interplay between the sexes. For Lawrence, each sex was defined with its own role; you had the masculine role if you were male, or you had the feminine role if you were female. It was another dichotomy. And despite his acknowledgment of a woman's power, throughout his work lurked the principle of female subordination to the male.

As I matured, I saw the sexes as interdependent, much like yin and yang. According to the Chinese philosophy, the two forces complement each other. Neither one dominates the other. Together, they form a whole. It seemed to me like such a civilized approach to the relationship of the sexes.

Sex was the most emphasized sin when I was in Catholic school. Once, my high school sponsored a series of lectures. Monday through Thursday the priest lambasted us about the evils of sex. Frankly, it got boring very early on. At last, on Friday, the priest talked about something else. His topic was gossip and the harm it could do. We were so glad to finally have something other than sex to think about.

Next to sex, the worst thing was lying to your parents. As a corollary to that, we were told "Never do anything that you wouldn't want your parents to see you doing." My teachers didn't know my parents. They could have been stumbling alcoholics or abusers or simply uncaring people. And why did the measurement of my goodness have to depend on someone else?

I took the injunction to be perfect very much to heart. No matter how hard I tried, there was always some standard that I fell short of, something I did wrong, something to confess. I was always striving for something I could never achieve. I was not supposed to get angry, become impatient, snap back at someone who'd hurt my feelings. When I failed at my bid for perfection, it meant I had sinned.

I was supposed to accept all the Church's teachings without question, and that troubled me too. One time, I was wrestling with a question, one I don't even remember now. I think it had something to do with the nature of Christ. Despite my prior experiences, I decided to ask my religion teacher about it. After all, we were in high school now. Some questioning would surely be tolerated. The nun was scandalized. "Do you doubt?" she asked me, her face stricken. Apparently, I wasn't free to doubt, to explore, to think for myself.

Absolutely nothing bothered me more about the Church than its patriarchal attitude. Even as a child, I was aware of it. My two brothers were altar boys. There were no altar girls. I must have been about nine or ten when I decided to write to the pope about it. Now, how did one address the pope? I couldn't just baldly ask my family. I didn't want anyone to know. I'd either scandalize them or suffer from their condescension or ridicule. Whatever their reaction, I didn't want it. So I started small, as if the subject were merely academic. "How do you address a monsignor?" "How do you address a bishop?" "How do you address the pope?" I got my answer.

Sitting at the tiny table in my room, I started to write my letter. I was consumed by the question: Why *couldn't* girls be altar girls? Then I realized something. When the pope answered me, the letter would come to my house. My parents and brothers would know. All my careful planning would be for nothing. I'd be exposed. Regretfully, I had to abandon my plan.

When I was growing up, it was taken for granted that only men were priests. They also, by the way, held the highest vocation. In descending order, the next highest vocations belonged to nuns, then married people, and then single people. That only a man could hold the highest vocation was never given a second thought, and was certainly never discussed. The older I got, the more I wanted to discuss it, and to change it.

And how did the nuns feel about having the second-best vocation, not because of any personal limitation, but because they intrinsically weren't worthy? How did they feel about, were they even aware of, the kind of sociological brainwashing that had been going on for thousands of years?

I grew tired of priests pointing out that the Blessed Mother was living proof that the Church recognized the importance and sanctity of women. It was going to take more than the Blessed Mother's elevated and revered status to counterbalance the misogyny in the Church, as far as I was concerned. The Church as an institution treated all women as second class. Then it pointed to its reverence for one solitary woman, to prove that it wasn't biased.

The Church's position on women bothered me more and more as I got older. I questioned the premise that women shouldn't have the same rights as men, and couldn't serve side by side as priests. One advocate of male-only priests argued that women couldn't be priests because there had been no female priests in Jesus' day. One could dispute that. Mary Magdalene comes to mind. And were there any Swedish priests in Jesus' day? Any Russians? Any Australians?

I had hoped that Pope John Paul II would change this restriction, but he made it quite clear that he wouldn't. When the pope died in 2005, I hoped and prayed that the new pope would change the Church's position. Pope Benedict XVI soon made it clear that the Church's position on women wasn't about to change on his watch. It would stay the way it had been for the past two thousand years.

I gave it a lot of thought. If this man didn't know as much as I did about the truth, how could I look to him as a leader? Could I wait for the next pope or the next to make things right? I had been a Catholic all my life. I had gone to Catholic schools. My parents had been religious, churchgoing people. My oldest brother was a priest. The Catholic Church was the only spiritual vehicle I had ever known. Could I leave all that over an issue that was clearly not important to the vast majority of other people, including so many other women? Including women in my own family?

It was wrenching to leave the Church in which I'd been raised, and had actively participated as an adult for so many years. It was wrenching to admit that I was so unseen by the Church. I would miss being a member of a spiritual group who believed in unseen dimensions to life, who professed love as its primary tenet, who lived by ideals, who believed that every moment of life held meaning. I'd also miss the familiarity of Church rituals, the mass, the Easter vigil service, the occasional smell of incense, the reading of the Gospel, the priests who put together a thoughtful sermon. I'd miss seeing the crucifix, the statues. I'd miss singing the hymns. I'd miss the familiar prayers. I would miss all that. And I would have to give up my own acceptance of an outer authority. I would have to go it alone.

My doctor recognized, more than I did, that leaving the Church was putting me under a great deal of stress. He suggested that I was looking for something like a father figure in the new pope, and that I had been left with no one to trust.

A father figure. It would be nice to have a father who cared for me and respected me at the same time, who allowed me to belong without believing that I was inferior, someone who understood me and could inspire me, clarify things for me, point out the way. That would be nice.

I finally made the break. Most of the pain and stress I felt came before I actually left the Church. Afterward, it was a little easier. I at least felt that I had done the right thing. But, all in all, the emotional upheaval no doubt contributed to my next psychotic episode.

As for the status of women in the Church, I've grown tired of arguing about it. When you come right down to it, the emperor has no clothes.

"You have to harness the energy
[of the episode] without letting it fry you."
Exactly.

Chapter 17

New York Hospital

I was thirty-four years old when David and I needed to move to a bigger place; we had a baby on the way. Looking for an apartment anywhere in Manhattan was out of the question, the rents being so high. We looked in other boroughs of the city, and wound up in Bay Ridge, Brooklyn. The new apartment was roomy; it had two bedrooms, a truly separate dining room (not a Manhattan alcove), a large living room, high ceilings, detailed molding on the walls, and a long hallway that we called the bowling alley.

I was happy to be in the new apartment, getting ready for the birth of our baby. I took some vacation time when we moved in, and delighted in emptying the moving boxes. Sometimes it was a four-box day, sometimes a six. I loved the sense of accomplishment, and the knowledge that I was preparing for Megan or Matthew, as the case might be.

I had been thrilled when my pregnancy test showed positive, and though I would have been happy to have either a boy or a girl, I fervently hoped for a daughter. It was an uncomplicated pregnancy. I had just the usual inconveniences—leg cramps, feet so swollen that the only shoes I could wear in the winter were Dr. Scholl's sandals along with heavy socks, feeling tired, a little morning sickness, and a craving for milk. I would wake up at two in the morning and fix a bowl of delicious cereal. At any hour of the day, I would drink a glass of milk—ambrosia.

When I first heard the baby's heartbeat, its rapid pulse reminded me of the enthusiastic panting of a puppy, as I told the doctor. "That's because you're glad to have the baby," he said. It made me feel so sorry for mothers who didn't anticipate having a baby with the same joy that I felt.

I was healthy throughout the pregnancy and at last, on an otherwise cold December night, I heard my doctor say, "You have a beautiful baby girl." David and I were thrilled with Megan, and, like new parents before us, told indulgent people more baby stories than they wanted to hear.

As for drinking milk, it was no longer ambrosia. I had been home from the hospital less than a week when I was having a bowl of cereal, only to look up, disappointed, at David, and say, "It's just milk, Dave."

The first few weeks after Megan was born, I was sleep deprived, and felt tired down to the very cells in my body. Who knew that such a tiny creature could be so much work? But, on the other hand, who knew that such a tiny creature could bring so much joy? I stayed home with Megan for the first four weeks. I was hooked. I knew that I wanted to spend more time with Megan than my full-time job allowed.

When I returned to work, I asked my boss if I could have more time at home. It wouldn't be year round, I knew that. We had our busy season from January through April. Taking time off then would be unthinkable, but I was hopeful that for the rest of the year we could work something out. "Would you like to work four days a week?" my boss asked me. I jumped at the generous offer.

I chose Wednesdays. That way I could prepare for being away on Monday and Tuesday, skip a day, and be back to handle things on Thursday. It wasn't as simple as just taking a day off, of course. I bought an answering machine (radical at the time, at least for me), stayed in touch with my secretary, and did some work from home. I squeezed in time during my commute, and worked extra hard the other days that I was in the office. It worked out well.

A whole day with Megan. What could be better? I stayed home, tended to her as an infant, and, as time progressed, we did projects, played with her toys, and read her books. The kitchen sink in our apartment had no cabinet underneath, so I could pull a chair up to the sink; Megan could sit on my lap, playing with the bubbles and washing the dishes with me. It was one of her favorite things to do. We'd go out shopping, and sometimes, as a special treat, we'd stop and get one slice of pizza that the man always sliced down the middle for us. We went on adventures to the city for special children's activities, like a play or story reading. I used to take her in her stroller, and many a kind man helped me up the subway stairs with it. They would usually say something, like, "Can I help you?" or "Would you like some help?" But my favorite was the older man in his undershirt who didn't say a word—just lifted the stroller up in his arms and brought it up the steps.

One particular Wednesday, when Megan was about a year old, I put her in her stroller and went out for a walk. I knew that nothing could have made me happier than I was at that moment. I thought about the job that let me have this extra time with her, and I knew that no briefcase brimming with documents could have made me feel more important. These moments with Megan were so precious that only someone in a similar situation could appreciate them. As we walked on, I passed another woman who was pushing her daughter in her stroller. The smile that she and I shared told me that she felt the same way.

Life continued with me in love with my growing child, in love with David, enjoying my work, discovering things about my neighborhood, and appreciating my large apartment, with its beautiful sunsets that I could see outside my kitchen window. I enjoyed these things for two and a half years after Megan was born. Then, I hit a snag. I was terrified that people could read my mind. I found myself lying on the bed next to David; he had his arm around me. I asked him if it was true. "No, nobody can read your mind," he said. A couple of minutes went by. Then I asked him again. He answered the same way. I kept asking him. Because I knew I could trust him, I could let a couple of minutes go by before I had to ask him again.

I wound up in the hospital. I had hoped to handle this episode the way I had the others—take some weeks off from work, spend more time with my therapist, take extra medication, strive to separate reality from insanity, and rely on the support of family and friends. However, this episode held some differences from the others. For one thing, I hallucinated, which was rare, as well as being particularly frightening. I had been standing in the kitchen, and had watched the raisins become cockroaches, and the Cheerios turn into worms.

After spending a couple of weeks at home, I checked myself into the hospital as a voluntary patient. I was admitted to New York Hospital's Payne Whitney Psychiatric Clinic, and stayed there for three weeks. The hospital's Abstract & Discharge Summary described first the "golden glow" period of my mania, when everything was easy and anything could be accomplished:

> *. . . this . . . female was functioning well at work and at home . . . until late February 1984 when she became increasingly energetic, describes her mood as 'terrific,' and was able to tackle previously burdensome workloads at her job with ease. In mid-March she withdrew $5000 from her savings account and spent it within the week on clothing. . .*

That euphoric stage never lasts very long and always deteriorates into full-blown mania. In mid-March I was spending money freely and having what I thought was a great time. By the end of March, I was psychotic, and on April 10th I was admitted.

> *Apparently two weeks prior to admission the patient began to 'unravel' – her thinking became disorganized and hyper-religious. She experienced auditory, visual and tactile hallucinations and delusions with religious, grandiose, and bizarre content . . .*

There was no ostensible reason for my life to "unravel." Although my job was stressful, it was also very satisfying. My home life could not have been better. I had a wonderful husband, and there was Megan, my greatest blessing.

What made that chemical imbalance I have kick in? Why does it ever kick in? If I took a wild guess, I'd say that it's similar to earthquakes. The fault line is the underlying cause for an earthquake, and I suppose that's what it's like for me. My chemical imbalance is my fault line, and my mental state is poised above it. Stress seems to trigger the chemicals, but they might get triggered after a long enough period of time anyway, even without the stress factor. But I really don't know.

I do know that the onset always hits me with a shock, that it gets very hard to remember the details of an episode afterward (much like trying to recall a dream that keeps slipping away), and that every single time it's over, I am sure it will never happen again.

The hospital report succinctly stated the reason why I had entered the hospital:

> *In anger, she thought fleetingly of murdering her husband and daughter by knife . . .*

It was an odd thought, murder. The thought appealed to me the way that a shiny object might appeal to a child. It had a seductive power that some remnant of my mind knew I had to fight against. I wasn't concerned about David. He was a big, strong man. But the thought of hurting Megan scared me in a way that I had never known before, and I entered the hospital so that she would be safe. Safe from me!

> *She described feeling that everyone could read her mind, that the news on TV and radio referred to her, that she was somehow responsible for the volcanic eruptions in Hawaii . . . and that she understood the book of Revelation.*

> *She hears frightening voices . . . , [has] strange tactile sensations, and visual hallucinations . . . She became frightened when she noticed crumbs of food on the table, saying, 'Everything seems to have special significance.' . . . Her judgement is clearly influenced by delusional thinking, but had some insight, asking for reassurance that her thoughts were not real.*

At New York Hospital, we met in groups, had dance therapy—where I remember crying—and group walks along the river. I liked the walks. I liked feeling less confined. I liked breathing fresh air.

We could associate freely with the other patients. We shared a certain camaraderie, an "us against them" mentality. One older man likened it to what he had felt on his submarine in World War II. We knew we were the different ones. We knew we had once been on the outside, where the staff still was, where our families still were. We knew what that felt like. But none of those outsiders could feel like us. They'd never know what our world was like. They'd always be on the outside. We had been in both worlds.

In college, I had heard of an experiment involving psychology students in grad school. They were admitted as mental patients into an institution. The staff never guessed that they were normal, but the other patients could tell. Was it a true story? I don't know, but it always fascinated me. If true, it meant that mental patients were still savvy, even if they were screwed up. That patients weren't fooled by the labels a society put on people. They had their own radar detectors, and they weren't taking anybody else's word for anything.

At the hospital, I became friendly with another patient, Lizzie. She never asked me what I was in for; I never asked her. It just wasn't proper etiquette. If some inmates wanted to reveal that they had tried to kill themselves, or had wandered, raving, out into the street, that was their business, but we never asked. Lizzie was pleasant and talkative. She talked about herself quite a bit, but she was charming and interesting, and she listened to me when I really needed her to. I learned that even a patient in a mental hospital could be a warm and enchanting person.

The day before I was to leave the hospital, Lizzie and I sat on one of the couches together and talked. I was excited to be going home—to be with David and Megan, to curl up with a cup of tea and a book whenever I chose, to watch TV, to listen to my music, to stay up late, to not have my behavior scrutinized, to make a tuna fish sandwich. I wanted to do all the everyday things that I couldn't do when I was behind locked doors, doors I couldn't open because someone else held the keys.

I talked with Lizzie about my excitement in leaving the hospital, and about the episode that had brought me there. The insanity had been so scary—all the delusions, the fear that people could invade my mind, trying to deal with people who were not who they purported to be, who were wearing disguises. Plus, the thought of murder and the hallucinations were particularly troublesome. "If I knew that I'd have another one of these," I told Lizzie, "I'd kill myself."

Later that day, I was called into the hospital office to see Richard, one of the staff members. He wanted to ask me a few questions. Richard was soft-spoken, dark-haired, thin, and always looked sincere. He reminded me of a seminarian. He indicated a chair to me, and I sat down. He told me that I'd been overheard talking about killing myself. My stomach cramped in fear.

I knew about the law that would allow a facility to keep me, without my consent, if it determined that I was a danger to myself or others. They could keep me for a short time while they made up their mind about me. If they decided that I wasn't a danger, they had to release me. But, if they decided that I was dangerous, then they could just keep me, indefinitely. They could keep me until I was no longer dangerous, which they were in sole charge of deciding.

There was a sign in the hospital about the few days that they were entitled to use for their evaluation, but I found it hard to understand when I was first admitted. Later, it made more sense, not that I ever thought it would apply to me. It applied to people whom I had studied in law cases; it applied to "other people," but it was merely of academic interest to me.

If I were sent to prison, I'd have a definite sentence. I could count the days until I'd be released. In the hospital, there would be no such end point. There would be only a "wait and see" day-by-day evaluation. In order to convince the hospital to let me out, I'd have to act "normal"—no rage, no frustration, no glum sadness at not going home. I'd have to act grateful that I was being looked after, perhaps a tad ashamed at causing so much trouble. I'd have to cooperate with whatever they said. Acting like that toward people who are keeping you confined against your will, and who have absolute power over you, isn't "normal." But it would be the only way out. The whole thing would be a challenging acting job.

Before I was called in to see Richard, I had been looking forward to going home the next day. In fact, I was thrilled. I wanted my freedom again, to hold my daughter again, to take a walk without permission. Even the possibility of spending "only" a few more days in the hospital seemed like forever to me. The thought was unbearable. If they decided I had to be in the hospital for longer than that, I didn't know how I would endure it.

I could have sworn that Lizzie and I had been alone in that corner of the room where we'd been sitting. Apparently not. Who could have told him? Maybe another patient, some goody-goody who wanted to butter up the staff. Now was not the time to think about that, however, and anyway it didn't really matter. I needed to focus on more important things. Now I had to reassure this man that I wasn't dangerous.

Strangely enough, Richard was nervous. I could see it, and I could hear it in his voice. That wasn't good. It would make him more defensive, less apt to see things my way. Richard was young. That wasn't good either. It meant that he hadn't had much experience as a professional. If he made the wrong decision, it could weigh heavily against him in his career.

And what was the right decision? If he decided to keep me in the hospital for evaluation, who would say that he was wrong? But if he let me go and I did kill myself, I would be a headline in the papers. The hospital would be blamed for letting me go—a mental patient with suicidal tendencies. He would be blamed for it. He'd feel guilty, and it would be terrible for him professionally.

I had to reassure him. It was "just an expression" that I had used, I explained. Of course I never meant that I would actually do such a thing. I knew I had a good life. I had a wonderful husband. I had a beautiful daughter, the joy of my life. I didn't have any intention of hurting myself.

I acted as if a verbal misunderstanding had occurred. I acted surprised at the conclusions being drawn from my little statement. It was just an expression of frustration. That was all. I was respectful to him. I didn't once get emotional. I didn't plead. I didn't raise my voice, cry, or show fear. I was calm, serious, and mature. By the end of the interview, I had convinced him. He told me that I was free to go home the next day. I rose from my chair feeling very proud of myself. Of course, I didn't let it show.

Trouble with nightmares again. Perhaps because of switching meds and fear of that.

Chapter 18

Medication

. . . she will be maintained on Lithium. Given past history of depression following her psychotic episodes, she should be watched carefully for symptoms over the next several weeks.

From the beginning, my doctor had encouraged me to take lithium. I wouldn't do it. I didn't need a drug in order to be normal. I could do it on my own. It was insulting to suggest that I go on drugs. It implied that I wasn't mature enough, or didn't have enough character, to handle myself. It meant that I was a weakling.

I know that there are people who don't believe in getting medical attention for anything, even something life threatening. I never felt that way. I had no trouble taking something for a bad headache or an upset stomach; I'd already had one operation and I had no qualms about having another if I needed it. My mind, however, was different. I didn't believe in taking any medication for my mind. My mind was myself, and I could take care of myself. I didn't see that the mind, when all is said and done, is part of the body after all. I didn't see it that way for quite a while.

I was sensitive to the stigma that society attached to my illness. Today, I'm a lot freer with saying that I'm bipolar. In fact, I'm rather proud of the fact that I've led such an ordinary, yet fruitful, life, all the while wrestling with that problem. But when I was younger, I felt differently. If I took drugs, it meant admitting that I had the illness, and that it wasn't going to go away. Taking drugs would mean that I was truly mad, unable to govern myself, unable to handle my life on my own. I would be a person who could be described as a basket case, or loony tunes, crackers, batty, nuts, demented, deranged, touched in the head, around the bend. Worse, I could be described as weak, immature, pathetic, feeble, pitiful. I wasn't going to allow it.

Despite my reluctance to go on medication, it was becoming increasingly obvious over the years that I needed help, and if that help was medication, then I'd better start taking it. My New York Hospital stay was my fourth episode in a span of eleven years. It was the second episode in which I had landed in a hospital. During the episode, I was a danger to my family, and I was hallucinating again. It didn't look like I was taking care of things all that well on my own.

Upon leaving the hospital, I agreed to go on lithium. I stayed on it for about a year, and then quit. The old thoughts still plagued me. I belittled the medicine as a crutch. I didn't need a crutch. Despite my doctor's urging, I was not a cooperative patient, and decided once again to handle the illness (really a "weakness of character") on my own.

It took a while before I entertained some new thoughts about being on lithium. Maybe handling the illness wasn't a question of maturity and character. Maybe it was just like any other biochemical abnormality. Maybe the illness was no more my fault than a broken arm would be. The pills were just another medication. I didn't expect my body to combat disease by itself. So why should I expect my brain to conquer disease by itself? Secretly, I still haven't fully resolved all my doubts. I'm concerned about being defective. About being damaged goods. No matter. Now I take more pills than just the lithium, and I take them regularly, morning and night, and on really bad days, I take some in between.

I've stayed on the lithium permanently. There are some drawbacks, though, the ever present side effects. Lithium slows my thinking, and makes it hazy. After a while it also gave me a tremor in my hands. The tremor keeps me from drinking soup in public, from carrying a teacup and saucer in one hand, and I absolutely can't do my nails.

After some years had passed, Depakote was added to the mix. Both lithium and Depakote were designed to even out the mood swings. The

Depakote had its side effects too. It slowed my thinking even more than the lithium alone, and added to the haziness. It also impaired my memory. David used to joke that he could take me to a favorite movie of his twice because I wouldn't remember the plot from the first time. Often, I would begin a sentence and forget where I was going with it. At work, I would forget conversations. I would go to phone somebody and have to stop and think—had I just done that? If I had done it, what had I said?

A lagging memory, a tremor in my hands that was perceived as nervousness, and difficulty completing my sentences because I couldn't hold on to the thought were disaster on the job. It was embarrassing as well. I took to eating sandwiches for lunch in the cafeteria. I could hold on to a sandwich with both hands, and the tremor wouldn't show. Using a fork or a spoon was more difficult. One person I knew told me he was relieved to find out that I didn't have Parkinson's disease.

The pills also made me tired. There were days at the office when I would close my door and nap during the lunch hour. Some days I couldn't do that, but I did it whenever I could. When I got home, I'd take another nap for an hour. I resented losing a part of my day to the little bottles that read, "May cause drowsiness. Use care operating a car or dangerous machinery."

After years on Depakote, I switched to a newer medication, Lamictal. The difference was noticeable within a number of weeks. I could remember things. I could start a sentence and then complete it. If I forgot where I put something, I could retrace my steps and find it again. I could understand what others were saying to me even if they talked in longer than three-sentence bytes. My memory will never be what it was premedication, but it is now more than serviceable. Coming out of that hazy fog was liberating. I no longer felt like my brain was stuffed with cotton wool. I wasn't tired all the time, as if I had taken a potent tranquilizer. I just got tired in the afternoon, then I took a nap and was fine. At work, I could run a department, supervise my staff, research the law, write memos, organize an eighteen-person team to deal with a substantive project, respond to my bosses' special assignments, and do it all with clarity and more energy.

In my medicine cabinet is a relative newcomer, Abilify, a mood stabilizer. At higher doses it also acts as an antipsychotic. It is key to stopping hallucinations. Needless to say, any pill that stops hallucinations is a favorite of mine.

Finally, there's Klonopin, a medicine for panic attacks. I felt personally insulted when I first started getting the attacks. I had the same feeling I'd had when I first became sick and refused drugs. I felt that the attacks were a negative reflection on my character. Panic attacks had never been my problem, but now it looks like they're here to stay. I'm told that many bipolar people develop something else besides the initial illness—something like obsessive-compulsive disorder or anxiety. The attacks resemble two things: a feeling of being so scared that I want to throw up, and a feeling of despondency, as if I'm sitting immobile in a chair, staring straight ahead at nothing. A panic attack combines the two. When not under full attack, there can be an underlying feeling of apprehension, something like nausea.

The panic attacks started suddenly and mysteriously. They were incapacitating. On one occasion, I sat all day in the rocking chair in my living room. Some unspecified fear took hold of me and I couldn't move. I had only one chore I wanted to do—trade in my old cable box for a new one—but I couldn't move from my spot. I was too terrified. Recently, I was sitting on the couch and I couldn't move, just sat there frozen, unable to do anything. I told myself to move, to do something that I was capable of, anything at all. I decided that I could do the dishes. After that I tackled the laundry. Next time, I know it won't matter how minor a task I start with, like sorting the mail or brushing my hair. It will help just to be able to move. I think.

When I have a panic attack, I often imagine all sorts of catastrophes, large and small. I imagine lightning coming through the air conditioner in our bedroom window, or that Megan will be hit by a car and be thrown into the air, that I'll fall down the steps in my house, that if I drive our car, I'll get into an accident, that the top of my electric toothbrush will fall off and go down my throat, that if I get gas put in the car, the attendant will go on fire. That last one is the one that made me think that my dire thoughts weren't really normal. Maybe something was wrong with me. And maybe my underlying formless apprehension wasn't quite normal either. Maybe they were worth mentioning to Dr. Schein.

I reported my feelings to my doctor, and was started on Klonopin, which gave me great, though not total, relief. Most of my current flashes of catastrophes resemble photographs that come to me briefly, rather than the way they did before, which was like watching a film that went on endlessly.

Then there are everyday worries. I worry about terrorists. I worry about being caught in the subway while a poisonous gas makes its way through the cars. I worry about Grand Central being blown up. I also worry about that particle bombardment they're doing underground in Switzerland; I worry about the radiation there. I classify these as normal worries, real-life worries that I have no control over. Things that pills can't take away. I tell myself to ignore them since I can't do anything about them. Besides, as far as the terrorists are concerned, "the best revenge is living well."

I have a sleeping pill, Ambien. It works fine. I'm not groggy the next day, and it brings me relief. I don't take it regularly, just when I feel I need it. I don't like the idea of taking sleeping pills often.

I take eighteen pills a day for the illness, prescription pills and over-the-counter supplements. They don't prevent episodes, but they do lessen the symptoms. They probably also lessen the frequency of the episodes, but that's impossible to tell.

I've increased my medication over the years, and all my prescriptions "may cause drowsiness." With my mild anemia added to the mix, I wind up napping, usually for two hours a day. I work my day around it, but there are some things that are difficult to do—go for a day trip to the city, take any all-day excursion, do anything that would prevent me from taking my rest in the middle of the day. It's another way bipolar disorder steals from my life.

The prescription pills are constantly warning me away from dangerous machinery. I manage to drive a car, taking care to drive in the early morning, or to have my nap beforehand, if need be. I do, however, stay away from tractors and any machinery that's taller than I am.

I am not my illness. Bingo.

Chapter 19

Postscript on Depression

After the mania is over, depression comes without fail. But there are times when its arrival has fooled me. Like depression, I get hay fever regularly, and, like depression, its arrival fooled me once.

Ever since I was twelve years old, I've had to put up with hay fever every spring. A few years ago, the trees were budding at their tips, but I had no symptoms. No burning, itchy eyes or itchy throat, no sneezing, nothing. I wondered why. Maybe a shift in my hormones was responsible for it, I thought. Whatever the cause, it was wonderful to be free of it.

Then the little tufts of pollen started falling off the trees. My eyes and throat began to itch. All the usual symptoms appeared. I was miserable. I still had hay fever; it was just waiting for the pollen to fall.

After a psychotic episode, depression doesn't always kick in right away. In my naiveté, I sometimes thought that meant I wouldn't have to suffer from it. I had a better understanding of my illness; that was it. I could stave off depression because I was more experienced now. It was wonderful to be free of it.

But it wasn't true. The depression was lurking all the while, just like my allergies, only waiting for the right moment to begin to make me miserable. After the insanity was over, depression might tantalize me by not showing up for a full week. I would be fooled, but it would inevitably arrive, like an unwelcome lover, hounding me for months.

Depression always comes with its lack of color and feeling, and its overwhelming exhaustion. Depression may have its roots in the mind, but some of its symptoms are definitely physical. The fatigue is physical. The inner nauseous feeling is physical. A simmering pain, like a poison eating at my insides, is physical. The need to sleep to avoid pain is physical.

Everything is tiring. Getting out of bed, walking, washing a dish, brushing my teeth, trying *not* to sleep—they all take enormous energy; they all feel pointless. A woman I knew, who had been hospitalized for depression, told me that someone had once asked her what she did all day. "I took a shower" was her reply.

If the depression is mild, I force myself to fight the exhaustion and do something during the day. Something more than spending my time sitting up, rather than lying down. Something more than avoiding multiple naps. One day I marshaled the effort to go to the pharmacy. That's all I did that day—no reading, no television, no shower. I was disappointed that all I had done was go to the pharmacy, but I knew I had to pat myself on the back just the same. I hate patting myself on the back for doing something I wouldn't even think about on a normal day. What I have to keep in mind is that it's not a normal day.

From the outside looking in, just getting through the day doesn't seem like anything difficult, let alone a major accomplishment. My aunt Muriel certainly didn't understand it. She thought that depression was weakness and self-pity. Every time I got depressed, she would say to me, "You see that world out there? Live in it!"

When she got older, she contracted emphysema. It tipped her into a depression. I empathized with her, and supported her emotionally as best I could. We talked daily on the phone, and I made the three-hour trip to her house when I could, and stayed for several days. I applauded her efforts, and let her know that I understood what she was going through. But I couldn't resist saying to her, just once, "See that world out there? Live in it!" She looked at me with recognition and remorse. She finally understood how cruel her words had been. After so many years, I had finally settled an old score.

Once, in the midst of a depression, I felt something that was far too pale to be called hope, yet had a vague resemblance to it. I was watching television. A man was tap dancing. He wasn't doing anything constructive, not building a building or fighting disease. He didn't even have a dance partner. He was dancing energetically all alone. He looked ludicrous.

In my depressed state, I thought that nothing mattered. *He* thought that that absurd dance mattered. I thought that death made everything meaningless; he didn't. I was amazed that he could defy death that way—that he could want to do something just because he wanted to do it, even if it was silly, even if its only purpose was just to *be*. Maybe, I thought, dying didn't make everything meaningless; maybe it just made living brave. The experience gave me something to think about that was outside the scope of my depression. I wondered about it from time to time.

Every depression drags on with no end in sight. I always get afraid that it will never leave me. It stretches in front of me, day after endless day. Can I possibly wait until it plays itself out? What if it never does play out? Some people are convinced that their depression will never end. They kill themselves rather than undergo unending suffering.

When depression is deep enough, suicide beckons enticingly. It would put an end to the suffering. Just knowing that I could do it gives me some relief. I wouldn't think of it as ending my life so much as I would think of it as ending the suffering. Forfeiting my life was just the price I had to pay. I've heard people say that suicide is an act of self-hatred. I can't agree. It's simply a way to end misery.

But whenever I've considered the practicalities, I've blanched. A gun? I would never touch a gun. Hanging? No, also too violent. Pills? What if I didn't swallow enough pills and I damaged my brain and became paralyzed? What if I didn't cut myself the right way in the bath? What if I botched the attempt and they put me in an institution? I could never think of a good way to do it. Even so, just mulling over the possibility was a comfort to me.

The misery of depression became too much for a friend of mine, who finally did kill herself. She had been on a series of antidepressive medications, but none of them helped her. I remember asking her about the latest medication she was on. Was it working; what would happen next if that one didn't work out? "Then I'll kill myself" was her answer.

I empathized with my friend of almost thirty years. I understood the hopelessness, the deadness, the bleakness, the despair. We talked about that. We were kindred spirits; I'd suffered as she was suffering; but my empathy was not enough. Still, every once in a while, I got a glimmer of hope when she gave a half-chuckle that was reminiscent of her laughter. Those were optimistic moments, but there weren't enough of them.

Now there's a vacuum where she used to be, not just in my life, and the lives of her family and friends, but in everyone's life that she would have touched. We're each of us something like a snowflake: unique, intrinsically beautiful, impeccably designed, impossible to duplicate. There's no replacing Denise.

When she had been healthy, mentally herself, she had embraced the spiritual, the joyous, the holistic, the organic. She enjoyed yoga and was a vegetarian. Denise was also very practical. When I first moved into my house, she came over and insisted on trimming the hedges. "I want to do something for you," she explained. She wanted to help hang pictures, to help me settle into my new home. She enjoyed being helpful. At times, she could be bossy about it, but given her generous nature, I knew she couldn't be anything but what she was. It was her idiosyncrasy, and I loved her for it.

We sang "Amazing Grace" at her funeral, and when I hear it now, I still cry.

Even the Tao says to undo.
If nothing is done, then all will be well.

Chapter 20

The Job

The psychotic episode following my graduation from law school, and the inevitable months of depression that followed, took almost a year out of my life.

When I could pretend to the world that my depression had gone away, I started to look for work. I sent out hundreds of resumes, got over a hundred rejections back. I'd get called for an interview, sometimes for a second or even third time. I'd come close, but I never clinched the deal.

My father was anxious for me to get started on my career. After one series of interviews, I got the word that I didn't get the job. My father called to ask if I had heard anything. Yes, I had heard; I didn't get it. "Bah," he said, and hung up on me. A little later he called back to explain that he had hung up because he was so disgusted for my sake that I didn't get the job. He wanted it for me so badly. I knew that already.

One of my more memorable interviews took place in a company's executive dining room. I had successfully passed muster with the two men I'd be working for. I'd had a second interview with each of them. I was then called back to meet the Top Boss. We arrived at the dining room, me in my forest-green interview suit. We were seated at the Top Boss's usual table. The waiter came over to take our order; I noticed his gold ID bracelet. I was sure it had cost more than my suit. The Top Boss, as was his usual prerogative, began to order lunch. The waiter interrupted. "Excuse me, sir. The lady first."

That was one of the jobs I didn't get.

It took me almost a full year before I was finally able to land what I considered a "real job," a job as a lawyer. It had taken a total of six years, between going to night school, recovering from my two episodes, and spending time looking for work, but I was a lawyer at last.

I would have been thrilled to be working either at a law firm or at a company with its own legal department. Anywhere, as long as it was a job. When I interviewed at the company I finally went to work for, one of the assistant general counsels asked me "Why don't you want to work in a law firm? You should work in a firm first. Get a little experience." It wasn't that I didn't want to work for a law firm. It was just that I hadn't been able to get a job there, or anywhere. I was desperate. I would have taken a job on the *Titanic*. I was totally unprepared for the question, but I managed what I hoped was a convincing song and dance about how I really wanted to work for a corporation.

I met with two other assistant general counsels, and the general counsel himself. Then I waited to hear. And waited. The personnel department (as it was called back then) was supposed to call me either way. My unemployment checks were due to run out soon. I was anxious. After several weeks had gone by, I mustered up my courage and called the personnel representative who had been assigned to me. Oh yes, I had the job, he said. There was just some paperwork that needed to be done, but everything was all set. I understood about paperwork, and sure enough there came a day when I walked into my office in my proper navy blue suit, ready to start work.

My first assignment confused me. I wasn't sure how my boss wanted me to approach it. David said, "If it were easy, he'd do it himself. He wouldn't need you." I tackled the assignment, with good results. My boss claimed it was "exactly" what he wanted.

I was glad to be working for a company, and not a law firm. I liked the benefits, and I liked the stock option awards. I liked working for a pharmaceutical company. We made medicines for people who needed them. We did tons of research. The company had a strong sense of ethics. We did something useful, unlike a candy manufacturer or some place that made perfume. That's the way I looked at it.

A couple of years later, I was rotated to work for another assistant general counsel, Tommy. We were a good team, and somehow I wasn't rotated again. My job involved devoting a third of the year to the one day in April when our company's annual meeting of shareholders took place. That four-month period was full of early mornings and late nights. "I'm coming back," I'd say to the security guard on the night shift, as I left the building to pick up some supper. Whoever was on duty would give me a wave and let me leave the building without having to sign out.

I drafted long, detailed legal documents in connection with the meeting. They had to fit within a framework of regulations so elaborate only a government agency could have thought them up. I prepared memos that went to all our top executives and all the directors on our board about their stock holdings, and aspects of their business associations. I also oversaw the printing and mailing of materials to our thousands of shareholders.

Details about the physical arrangements—how many shareholders to expect at the meeting, and scheduling times for the rehearsals of the executives' speeches, and so forth—also had to be nailed down. In between preparations for the meeting, a crisis that had to be solved right away was always cropping up. Time was tight, hours long.

I began to accumulate assistants as I took on more and more of the annual meeting responsibilities, as well as being responsible for other areas, including our department for shareholder relations. Random projects were always par for the course. My staff was terrific. Two lawyers, two paralegals, and my admin were all top-notch—intelligent, focused, collegial, and professional.

Despite the help, it was still a heavy workload. During one hectic period, my boss came into my office and told me of an assignment he wanted me to handle. I had been working at full throttle. I couldn't work any harder than that. I actually put my head down on my desk, looked up, and said only two words: "I can't." It was the only time that I refused an assignment. He seemed a little amused that I hadn't accepted a project with my customary poise. He said, "That's all right. I'll handle it."

I often worked into the night. When I worked past dark, I liked to see the patterns that the lights made in the windows of the buildings around me. Other cities might have their nights, and their buildings, and their lit windows, but only New York was a woman, dark and elegant, with diamonds at her throat.

Many times, when I'd finally get home from work, David would say, "God, you look tired." After another long night, he'd say the same thing. I finally asked him, "Can't you wake up early one morning, and say 'God, you look good'?"

Personal life was crammed into after-work hours and what was left of the weekends. Being half of a working couple meant that arrangements for picking up dry cleaning, or being at home for the plumber, had to be juggled with care. Mostly I missed my time with Megan. I missed her every time I had to work late, and every time I had to work on a weekend. Meanwhile, David took care of picking her up from the babysitter and cooking dinner. I tried hard to get home for dinner, but often missed it. My dinner was often a soda and a slice of pizza at my desk, from the pizza place around the corner.

If I did get home on time, David would have already cooked supper. I'd get up at the end of the meal to wash the dishes. That was our system. If I cooked, he did the dishes. If he cooked, I did them. Many times Dave would lumber out to the kitchen and start the dishes even though it wasn't his turn. "Dave, you don't have to do that," I'd protest weakly. "Do you want to do them?" he'd ask, teasing me. I would stay put and count my blessings.

I left in the morning before Dave and Megan were awake, usually 5:45. I caught the express bus into the city, getting a little more sleep along the way. Any later than that, and the bus would get caught in traffic, and I wouldn't be saving any time. I'd take the subway instead, a one-hour-and-twenty-five-minute ride. It was never an hour and a half; it was exactly that twenty-five minutes. Unless I heard the too-familiar "We apologize for this delay" announcement, and then it was anybody's guess how long it would be. At night, I often worked late enough to get a company car to take me home. No traffic problem at that hour either.

With my high-strung temperament, I was lucky to be working for Tommy, who was known for his even disposition and unruffable manner. Nothing fazed my boss. He was the one who would always say during a crisis, "It will work out. It always does." He believed in putting family first, and his religion was central to him. In all the nineteen years I spent with him, I heard him curse exactly once. A few of us were standing outside his office when we heard him say "goddamn it" into the phone. We stared at one another in disbelief, eyes wide, jaws dropped.

Not that he never got angry. I once had to tell my boss some bad news, for which I was responsible. I had let something rather important slip through the cracks. The mistake didn't just reflect on me; he wouldn't look good either if we didn't find a way to fix it. When I got home, I told David about it.

"What did Tommy say?" David wanted to know.

"Well, he didn't really say anything," I replied, "but he did raise an eyebrow at me."

"Wow!" said David. "Tommy must've really been angry with you!"

As a rule, though, my boss was quite pleased with my work, and my career progressed. I was given good raises; I got promotions; I got more responsibilities. I started doing assignments for my boss's boss, also a lawyer. I called him "Mr. D." I sometimes called him by his first name, but I liked "Mr. D." It had the right combination of regard and familiarity to it. I worked hard for both of them. As Mr. D liked to say, "The reward of good work is more work."

One Saturday, my boss and I had to come in to the office to work on a project. As luck would have it, David had to work that day too. I told my boss that, for lack of childcare, I'd be bringing four-year-old Megan with me. When Megan and I arrived, Tommy came out of his office holding a plastic bag, which he gave to Megan. Inside were a Yosemite Sam coloring book and a box of crayons. I knew that he had just bought them at a store up the street. He'd bought them himself. No wife.

When the annual meeting season was over, I could breathe more easily. The rest of the year wasn't as hectic. For the most part, I stopped eating lunch in my office, stockpiling trays from the cafeteria under my desk. During the off-season I was able to gather with the other attorneys for lunch. We talked a little about work, mostly about what was going on in our lives, our kids' lives, and life in general. There was some talk about sports, but not too much.

The cafeteria workers took good care of us. I was a regular; they knew what I liked and how I liked it. In the morning I had a bialy, lightly toasted, for breakfast. One morning it came out of the toaster very dark. I went to reach for it, but the server refused to set it on the counter for me. "No, no," she said, "I know how you like it," and she put a fresh bialy in the toaster.

From time to time, I would bring Megan to work with me. I would bribe her with a new book, and throughout the day be charmed by the sight of her perched on my broad windowsill, reading. She was also happy to make copies and, at a younger age, to string paper clips together.

One of the days when I brought her to work turned out to be about the busiest I'd ever had. I dashed around solving problems, writing documents, taking phone calls, conferring with my boss. Ten-year-old Megan saw me on the phone, simultaneously rifling through papers on my desk and waving someone in so I could sign some documents. Later, she said, "No wonder you're so tired!" I was touched that she appreciated the workload that caused me to be so tired when I got home. She understood that I had *reason* to be tired; I wasn't innately frail. I was tired because the job took a lot out of me. I told the story to my aunt Muriel. "And that's your Oscar," she said.

Every three years on average, a psychotic episode meant that I had to take a number of weeks off from work. My boss would encourage me to take all the time I needed. "Your health is more important," he used to say, and I knew he meant it. Mr. D made a point of assuring me that my recurrent absences didn't affect my advancement possibilities. He said he thought no more of my time off than he would of my taking time off for the flu.

In my latter years with the company, I found the workload and the pressure more and more difficult to handle. I had had multiple episodes, which were wearing me down. On top of this, I contracted a serious case of anemia. At first the doctors didn't know what caused it. For a while they were leaning toward cancer. I didn't want to be sick; I didn't want to die. I didn't want to leave Megan at her young age of sixteen. Many times I would tell myself to stop worrying, and to leave it up to Providence. For a few moments this would work fine, and I'd feel more relaxed. But in no time I'd start to worry again.

Meanwhile, I was getting progressively more tired. I was dragging myself around everywhere, and work was no exception. I asked Tommy if I could work three days a week, and two at home. The next thing I knew, both my bosses were in my office, offering me another option. They both believed that I should not try to work while I was sick. As Tommy had said to me a few times before, "Your health is more important." If I was too sick to do the job right, then I should take disability leave, find out what was wrong, and get well as soon as possible. Then I could come back to work with the drive and enthusiasm they expected of me.

I was lucky that by this time we had moved out of Brooklyn and into a house in the suburbs. It was summer, and because the anemia made me cold, I doubly appreciated the summer heat. I loved being in our new town. I enjoyed its many flowers and trees, and its sweet-smelling air. The world was no longer mostly cement. My world had always been mostly cement. As a child, I had wondered about the dust kicked up by the ballplayers whenever my father watched "the game" on television. I never saw so much dust on our sidewalks. At my first live baseball outing, I saw that the paths between the bases weren't cement; they were dirt. No cement? What a surprise.

I loved living in a house—no loud upstairs neighbors to contend with. I loved living in a small, quiet town where nothing much happened. I loved the backyard that David made so beautiful. I loved not taking the subway to work—loved not saying to myself, whenever I saw a strange person in the subway car, *Please, God, don't let him sit next to me.* I loved the fact that I could walk everywhere—to the library, to Church, to the train station, to the pharmacy, the deli, and the diner.

That summer, though, I didn't walk around much. I spent hours outside in the backyard, resting in the warmth of the sun, and the peace and quiet of the yard. I often said a silent thank you to God that we had moved out of the city. If I'd still been in Brooklyn, I wouldn't have a backyard. I would have been confined to the apartment instead. When summer ended in September, I felt so cold that I always wore my red down winter coat inside the house. I wasn't able to do much, but I told myself that I would do at least one thing each day. Something active, not just rest and sleep. One day the chore I set myself was to bring a screwdriver from the basement up to one of the bedrooms. I wanted Megan to tighten a bracket on the curtain rod. In the morning I got the screwdriver from the basement to the first floor. Then I had to rest. I napped for a couple of hours. Then I took the screwdriver up to the bedroom. Then I had to rest again. I napped for a couple of hours. Other than napping, I rested all day, sitting on the couch wearing that red coat. That was my accomplishment for the day—retrieving a screwdriver. It was all that I was capable of. Other days mimicked that one, but that one was the worst.

One day I was sitting at one end of the couch; Megan was at the other. David came home from work. He asked about the results of some tests that the doctor had taken. I told him it wasn't encouraging news. I saw both Megan and David slump forward, as if I had dealt them a blow. That's what made me realize that my sickness was taking a toll on them. They were also affected by my situation, because I was important to them, because they loved me. I really hadn't considered that before. My heart went out to them, especially to Megan who was so young at the time, just sixteen.

Three doctors were involved in my case. They held conference calls with one another: the hematologist/oncologist, my internist, and my psychiatrist. I had a bone marrow test. The lab wasn't pleased with the sample, so I had to have another one. The doctors tried different combinations of medicines, even taking me off one of my bipolar medications for a while.

Every time a medicine or dosage was changed, it would take several weeks before they could determine if the new combination could eliminate the anemia. Eventually, their hunch was proved right; the anemia was drug related. They did finally find the right combination of drugs, but even so, I would always remain mildly anemic.

I am always colder than anyone else in the room. If I go to a restaurant or the movies in the summer, when the air conditioning is on, I'm amazed that people in short sleeves are comfortable, while I'm better off with a sweater or a jacket. I also tire easily. It's a far cry, however, from the state I was in before the right pharmaceutical combination was found. After that, it didn't take long before I was able to go back to work.

When I returned to work after months on leave, everything was just as stressful for me as it had been before I left. I began to dread coming into work. I dreaded that feeling of fear in my stomach when the inevitable crisis came up. I dreaded answering the phone, not knowing what I'd be questioned about. I became increasingly anxious and decreasingly productive. The stress made me more and more nervous. Finally, I could no longer function in the job, and I went out on disability leave.

My boss was surprised. He thought that things were working out well. He was disappointed to find out that he was wrong. He didn't know the effort it took for me to come to work, and the stress I felt from working at all. In the end, he was as sympathetic as ever. He predictably said, "Your health is more important."

Mr. D wasn't surprised. He told me that he had seen it coming. "I thought this was going to happen," he said. "I didn't want it to happen, but I expected it to happen." I was ashamed at not being able to handle the job anymore, but he encouraged me to think of my disability as just that, a disability, and not a personal failure. I was grateful for his understanding.

Considering the nature of my illness, it helped that I worked at a pharmaceutical company. Nearly everyone understood that chemistry could affect both the body and the mind. My illness was treated *as* an illness, not as a sideshow. But mostly, I was lucky to have worked for my boss and Mr. D.

Usually after a manic phase, I get depressed —
nature's clumsy way of narrowing the
access to an altered state.

Chapter 21

Theories

Sometimes, my subconscious takes over my life. My rational mind is nowhere to be found. My actions are dictated entirely by subliminal motives. I am swimming in an ocean of subconscious thought. That's insanity. Anyhow, that's how it seems to me.

The subconscious thought patterns of my dreams and the thought patterns of my insanity have much in common. One of the most important is a feeling—a slow-motion, underwater feeling. Other things they have in common: in both states, time is distorted; two contradictory things can happen at once; symbolism is extensive; and hallucinations can occur.

The relationship of how we dream and how mania operates also caught the attention of Sigmund Freud. He thought that studying the subconscious through dreams would help to understand madness and vice versa.

During an episode, I sometimes feel like I'm slogging through the atmosphere, the way I feel in a nightmare when I can't run fast enough. Things seem hazy; they're in soft focus. Dreaming, I sometimes struggle to wake up out of a nightmare. Struggling through insane thoughts can feel the same way.

Another similarity is that of substituting one person for another. When I'm psychotic, I often think that one person is really another in disguise. I might think that the police sergeant is really my father, masquerading as the sergeant. In the symbolism of dreams, a person is often not really himself. Instead, he is merely acting as a camouflage for someone else. In both cases there is a cover-up; things are not as they seem.

When my subconscious creates dreams for me, it does an imaginative and helpful job. As the source of my creativity, it brings me great joy. But when it rules my waking life, the result is disastrous. It is not equipped to manage everyday events. It has no conception of boundaries, no idea of limits, no thought of self-restraint. Left unattended, the incredible force of my subconscious can blow me away, like blowing the cover off a manhole. Without my rational mind to stop me, my impulses have no filter. I go straight from subconscious desires into action. I engage in bizarre behavior; I shock people; I act outside social mores. Without the rational mind to direct my thinking, I am inundated with terrifying thoughts. I become delusional.

My rational mind may not be the creative genius that my subconscious is, but it has its uses. It judges my delusional fears and reassures me that they are not valid. It judges my actions and decides what type of behavior is acceptable. It prevents me from stripping off my clothes and walking naked down the street. That would not be appropriate, it would tell me. It would instruct me not to go up to total strangers and link arms with them while they're walking along. Not to walk down the street yelling at the top of my lungs.

My useful rational self filters everything in my life to and from my subconscious. It maintains my creative energy at a workable level, so I am not losing my needed sleep. It keeps from me an otherwise overwhelming number of ideas, and lets me be aware of them in manageable portions.

Despite its contributions, when my rational mind is in sole charge of my psyche, that, too, is disastrous. In fact, I hold my rational mind responsible for the depression that inevitably follows my psychotic episodes.

When I'm sick physically, my body tries to heal itself. When I'm sick mentally, my mind tries to heal itself. If my subconscious is responsible for the madness, then one sure way to bring the madness to an end is to shut off all access to that area. If my subconscious is no longer dictating my life, then there is no more crazy behavior. This is where the rational mind steps in. It stops the madness by shutting down access to the subconscious and taking over the psyche completely.

Unfortunately, when that access is shut down, so is all access to creativity, spontaneity, joy, and passion. Not having contact with the creative areas of my nature leaves me without excitement, pleasure, or enthusiasm. With the subconscious totally out of reach, there is no meaning to life. I become depressed. But at least I'm not mad. Nature's use of depression as a method to heal the mind is clumsy. The cure is almost worse than the disease.

I think about reality often—what it is, and, importantly for me, how to perceive it. When I'm not sane, I have trouble knowing whether a person is who he appears to be; whether that person is trying to trap me; even whether those birds are trying to tell me something. How can I know the answers to these things when my knowing apparatus has been shot to smithereens?

After I've moved on from total insanity, and I'm on the mend, I realize how wrong my thinking process has been. This goes way beyond merely making mistakes. This is fundamental. It goes right to the core of what I am. It's about how, not what, to perceive. How can I fathom what's real and what isn't when the "I" that's judging is so fragmented? I know I can't trust myself. Then who can I trust? What can I trust—what idea?

I hate this aspect of the madness. I feel totally alone. I can't choose someone else as a reality check. I have no basis on which to make that decision. How can I rely on Doctor X or President Y or Religious Leader Z? In order to rely on them, I would first have to use *my judgment* to decide that they're right. Authority figures don't just crop up out of nowhere; I have to anoint them. It all leads back to me.

I can't choose a structure for myself, but I'm lost without one. I can't fold myself into the Church structure that my mother found comfort in, or the army structure my brother Kevin thrived in. My psychiatrist gives me something of a structure. David, too. I need more, though; I need something to hold on to besides the twisted thoughts that swirl in my head, and the nightmares that come when I go to sleep.

Do normal people have bad days
only when something bad happens?
Wow.

Chapter 22

Nightmares

My nightmares are usually about bugs, sometimes snakes, even raccoons. How can something as small as an insect be so threatening? Why not dream about a charging rhinoceros? I never have dreams about big animals.

I dreamed once that a person was standing with three large black insects on her—one covering her face, the other two covering the rest of her head. I brought the dream to Dr. Schein. He interpreted it to refer to the three bosses I had at the time, and the stress of the job. That made sense to me. Stress frightens me, not in and of itself, but because I know where it can lead.

Another time, I dreamed about one of my pills. It had hairy legs and was walking across my hand. Then there was the one about the white fence and one, then two insects walking across it. Some time ago, I dreamed that one wall of my apartment was completely filled with roaches, rushing up the wall. At the time, I was convinced that the dream was prophetic and that I would experience it in real life.

Recently, I dreamed a spider was inside my body. Besides the unnerving presence of these insects and animals, there's something different about the quality of these creatures. They're not ordinary. They have a bizarre power about them, an intelligence, an intention.

I've dreamed that an army of mice or rats was scampering across the floor, chasing a small child. Sometimes, when I've had a string of these, I pray to my subconscious before I go to sleep, *Please, no nightmares.*

Occasionally, when having one of these dreams, I'll moan aloud or sit up in bed. David will put his hand on me and say, "I'm right here." It amuses me a little that his response is not "It's all right," but rather that he's there. That his being there should take care of it. It doesn't, but it helps.

They say the average person has three nightmares a year. I'm way past my quota. Besides the nightmares making me afraid to go to sleep, I have another problem with sleep, insomnia. When I first heard that people had insomnia, I thought it must be a lot of fun. To be up in the middle of the night, when everyone else is asleep. To take a walk in the solitary dark, to go out to an all-night diner.

It's not like that.

I wake up anywhere from two to four a.m. and lie there for an hour or so, staring at the ceiling, hoping I'll go back to sleep. I don't. Then I go downstairs. I fix a cup of tea, and settle down on the couch to watch television. I prefer infomercials. I find it very relaxing to watch people promote a product that I could never use. There's no pressure to buy; I can just sit back and watch all the happy, upbeat people. Plus I don't have to follow a plot. Whether it's a face cream, or a special vitamin drink, or an exercise machine, it really doesn't matter to me.

Second on my list are old movies, especially glamour movies from the thirties or hard-boiled mysteries from the forties. I don't read, because reading takes concentration, and I don't have enough of that.

I do have the Ambien for when I have trouble falling asleep. The pills are very helpful, but they're useless at four in the morning. No, at that hour of the day there's nothing to do but to slug it out. Three hours or so later, I go back to bed. The next day I'm a little off-kilter.

You only get past things when you realize you don't need them, at which point you have passed them already.

Chapter 23

After the Job

At first when I took disability leave from my job, all I wanted to do was rest. I planned to have a full year of total relaxation, no obligations. I planned to wake up and do anything I wanted, or not do anything at all. I took everything slowly. It didn't take much to engage my attention—a walk in the neighborhood, the leisure to stop and admire the flowers, a trip to the library, lunch with a friend. Before a month had gone by, however, another episode interrupted my plans. Why was this happening when I had left the pressure of the job behind me?

My doctor's opinion was that job pressure may have been one factor in having these episodes, but being without a job was another. For twenty-one years, I'd held a job that was fulfilling, challenging, something I could be proud of. I used to love to say, "I'm a lawyer," whenever anyone asked me what I "did." Without a job, I lost my distinctiveness. I had taken such pride in being a lawyer, and now that was gone. Now I was just me. Of course, I was always "just me," but leaving the job meant leaving behind the proof that I was capable and intelligent.

Once I left the job, my routine changed dramatically and abruptly. I no longer had the structure of office life—having a place to go to where I belonged. I no longer had my schedule, my easy commute, the camaraderie of my colleagues, the sociability of the secretaries, the cafeteria lady who knew just how I liked my bialy. I missed answering the phone with my full name, and I even missed choosing which of the pairs of shoes hidden under my desk I would wear that day. As for the intellectual challenge, I missed that, too, but not right away. I was too tired. Missing that came later.

Along with missing certain aspects of the job came disappointment in myself. I hadn't stuck it out; I had given in to the exhaustion and stress, given in to the fragility of my psyche. Why couldn't I manage? How could I let myself be overwhelmed, incapacitated? Why couldn't I be like other people? I had an illness, yes, but why couldn't I handle the stress of ordinary life? Granted the stress level was high at the job, but other people didn't fall apart like I did. Somehow I should have persevered. Instead, I had failed.

I also felt that I was a disappointment to the memory of my deceased father, who had been so proud of my being a lawyer. He and I had both worked at the same company, our careers overlapping for a few years. He used to love to introduce me to his colleagues as his daughter *and* a lawyer.

He was a company man, dedicated to the corporation where he had worked for more than thirty-five years, and taking pride in doing his job the very best way he could. He aimed for perfection, regularly achieving it. As he often said, "If you're going to do something, do it right." He was professional in everything he did. I felt disloyal for giving up the work world, for not pushing myself further, for not following his example of working at the company until full retirement.

Whatever the reasons for it, the episode happened. As these things go, it was a mild one. I muddled through, feeling like my delusional thoughts were sticky glue that I kept getting caught in. Some of the delusions were basically repeats from earlier episodes. Others were more novel.

I became convinced that a teacher I had had thirty years earlier was really a guru, a secret guru who was on earth to impart ultimate wisdom without my realizing it. I wondered if he was able to read my thoughts back then. I wondered if he could read them now. I would talk myself out of that idea, and then find myself thinking it again.

Other potential gurus came to mind. In each case I wrestled with the possibilities, sometimes believing them, sometimes breaking free of the magnetism of the thoughts. No hallucinations, but still a twenty-four-hour fight. I was angry at having fallen into this trap once again. One night

I wrote about the psychosis: "Someday [I will] put my hands around its throat, and choke the life out of it."

I recovered. For some reason, I didn't suffer from depression to any great degree. When the episode was over, I resumed my original plan of relaxation. I had lunch at the diner in the company of the crossword puzzle. I moved around in the day with an ease and freedom that were new to me.

After about a year, I started to do things. Bridge lessons were offered in my community. I had tried learning the game twice before, but I couldn't get the hang of it. Bridge was a foreign language to me, and I didn't speak it. Remarkably, through my community's bridge lessons, I finally learned to play the game. I'm sure it was due entirely to the clarity, humor, and patience of my teacher.

I began playing with the seniors in my town, many of whom had been playing for years. They were patient as I learned, and helpful with the finer points, once I got past the basics. The seniors remain a great source for movie reviews; they update me on community affairs; they advise me on everything from who's a good plumber to where to buy wholesale jewelry.

I joined a women's club, a very sociable group. Although its aim is to raise funds for local charities, they make sure to have fun along the way. I joined their bridge group. They hold a tournament and, at the end of the year, charming prizes are awarded, including a prize for the lowest ranking team, an honor that my partner and I achieved one year.

The club's gourmet group is another favorite of mine. Each member takes a turn hosting a dinner, and guests arrive with dishes to supplement the hostess's entrée. Our conversation is wide-ranging. I was surprised the first time politics came up. These ladies have strong opinions and don't mind flatly contradicting someone else's point of view. Even though they don't mince their words, it still doesn't get in the way of laughing with each other afterward, getting on with other topics of conversation, and sharing knowledge and advice. We enjoy the food, the wine, and one another.

I was invited to join another women's club. Members choose a topic each year, and then each member is assigned an aspect of the topic, which she is expected to research and report on. I've learned things about the transcontinental railroad, Islamic law, and Cecil Rhodes. About Darwin, Freud, and Einstein.

When I first joined the club, I was intimidated by the women's intelligence, their education, their knowledge of current events, and their frequent travels to out-of-the way places. They made me feel at ease over time, and I've learned how generous they can be, whether it's offering a ride home, or sharing an article, a book, a film, that might be helpful to someone's topic.

When a friend of mine was involved in assigning topics for the following year, she asked me, "I think, for the first presentation, that we should start with the fall of Constantinople in 1453 and continue up to Napoleon's conquest of Egypt. What do you think?"

Ask me when Columbus "discovered" America, and I can be of some help, but not with the relationship of Constantinople and Napoleon. I was amused that she would assume that anyone would naturally be able to engage in a dialogue on the subject. I told her that I couldn't help her. "Martha, I would love to help you, but I don't know anything about it." She looked at me curiously, like I was an odd little creature, but didn't press the matter.

The two clubs bring me into needed social contact. I've made some friends there, as well. David has become used to my referring to them as "my women."

When acting lessons were offered in my town, I signed up, thrilled at the opportunity. Lessons from acting spill over into my real life. I hear my acting teacher's voice saying: "Stay in the moment." "That's the old moment. Be in the new moment." "Don't move unless you have to." "Don't speak unless you have to." And more. I find it all very Zen. The trick is to get on the stage without my ego, without any of "oh, they're looking at me" rattling around in my head. If the audience can see "me," that is, my ego, my persona, then I'm not doing my job. If they see my soul, that's okay. A lot easier said than done. I learn, keep learning, despair of learning, get happy because I am learning, and so it goes.

A friend enlisted me in a writing workshop. I was amused that she just enlisted me, without even asking. Her zodiac sign is Leo. I guess that explains it a little. The group meets biweekly as a rule. We read and dissect different types of writing: poems, mysteries, children's stories, nonfiction, romances, and even an epic novel set primarily in Russia.

In my classmates, I find insightful and uncensored criticism for my writing. Unlike the performing arts, a writer can't know her audience's immediate reactions to her work, but reading aloud to the group gives me the uncommon opportunity to get my readers' reactions firsthand. I find out what they liked, what they disliked, and what parts were unclear. We also happen to have a grammatical expert in the group, who advises on capitalizations, the placement of quotation marks, commas, and the like.

The group offers encouragement and incredible support and good will. I am gratified that, even with months going by in between, they remember details from a previous chapter of my work and relate them to a new piece I am presenting. We are all grateful for our teacher, who offers deft editing, incisive comments, and unparalleled dedication. She not only is, but looks, creative, with a remarkable collection of original jewelry, which she wears with impeccable flair.

I have friends I lunch with, go to the movies with, have conversations with.

Once a week I meet Megan in the city for dinner. She greets me with her customary effervescence, and a kiss. At dinner, she is quick to laugh, and at other moments, quick to cry. I admire that she is also quick to forgive. She delights me, comforts me, engages my intellect. She offers telling comments about the people we know, and even about people I talk to her about, but whom she's never met.

I once told her, "I can see the passion in you. It's as if your skin is translucent, and I can see the flame inside." She has always been the joy of my life, at every age. She remains so now. She's my prayer.

Megan has seen me on my worst days, my bad days, and my good ones. She told me once that a line from a movie reminded her of me. It was something to the effect that nothing in particular had to happen in order for the woman to have a bad day. Her understanding comforts me.

She once witnessed one of my shopping sprees. It was during a two-month period when I had spent an enormous amount of money—$10,000. I still wince at both the waste and the lack of control. She was a teenager at the time, and I took her shopping with me to a large department store.

I kept piling my cart with everything I liked, from a rubber ducky to sheets and towels and placemats and napkin rings and kitchen utensils, and charming, impractical items. Megan suggested that I was buying too much, but no, I was happy; this was fun; things were pretty; things were cute.

She couldn't stand to watch and wanted to leave and go sit in the car. She asked me for the keys. No problem. She left and I went back to my shopping.

After a while she came back and I was delighted to show her a really adorable clock that lit up when you touched it. She had seen me enough times to know what my frenzied shopping meant. "It was scary," she told me just the other day.

How many times, and how deeply, have I scared her? I would spare her anything, if I could. I would spare her my illness. I would spare her any pain, absorb it as my own. I would die for her.

A couple of years after I left the job, I got a notice from my disability insurance company that I was to be interviewed by one of their psychologists. At issue was whether I could hold down a job, any job. The notice said that I should bring a pair of sneakers with me. I knew that it was a form letter, and that my disability didn't waver whether I had sneakers on or not, but I didn't want to do anything wrong, so I brought them with me.

I didn't know quite what to expect. I wasn't looking forward to being scrutinized, and I was petrified of the possibility that the insurer's psychologist would find me fit for work. I knew I wasn't. I knew how worn-out I was during my last months at the job. I would come home exhausted and the first thing I'd do would be to take a nap. When I woke up, I'd eat dinner, enjoy a cup of tea or two, then go to sleep. I'd do it all again the next day. The responsibility of the job, and the stress that came along with it, left me feeling like a boxer who had had too many bouts. I knew I couldn't handle it. Would the psychologist agree?

I had to go to New Jersey for the interview. I am a very tense, not to mention unskilled, driver. I never drive on parkways if at all possible. If I find myself on one, I start to sweat. Going to New Jersey was way beyond my league. I suppose the insurance company thought it was being considerate by giving me a neighboring state. I never thought to ask them if I could go to Manhattan instead. I thought of it the next time though.

David drove me to the interview. He found a park to walk in while he was waiting around for me. The interview lasted almost six hours. I gave a history of my illness, which dredged up unpleasant memories and left me a little shaky. I answered many multiple-choice questions like "in this situation I usually . . . " My IQ was tested, and I had to duplicate shapes (not my strong point).

I waited anxiously for the results. I was relieved to learn that he found me disabled.

A few years later, I received a similar notice. This time I asked for the interview to be held in Manhattan, and it was. In this interview, to my surprise, I could duplicate shapes more accurately and quickly than I would ever have thought myself capable of doing. He tested my vocabulary; it was stellar. I asked the psychologist as I was leaving, "If I were an intelligent woman, would that be held against me?"

"Oh, you are, you are," he assured me, but went on to say that there were other factors involved. As it turned out, he also recommended against my returning to work. I was relieved and grateful, but, human nature being what it is, I felt a little insulted each time.

I've stopped keeping exact track of how many episodes I've had—there have been too many of them, for one thing, and I like to forget about them, for another. But I do mark milestones. I lasted five years without one, from 2000 to 2005, a long time for me. Then it came.

At the time, I was having medical problems. Courtesy of my maternal grandmother, I now had arthritis. It settled all along my spine, resulting in painful muscle spasms from my shoulders to my hips. I went to physical therapy three times a week. On top of that, I had pain in both my ankles (damaged ligaments and a sprain). I had pulled the muscle behind my right knee, and had to get an MRI on the other knee. I had tendonitis in both my wrists. No matter how I moved, I was in constant pain.

I kept a chart of when I had taken the pills for the pain, what times I had put the heating pad on, ditto the ice packs, and when the antipain patch went on and off. At night, I took a sleeping pill, not because I needed it mentally, but because no matter what position I tried lying in, I was in too much pain to sleep. I couldn't take my usual afternoon nap, which I needed both because of the "may cause drowsiness" pills I was taking, and because of my mild anemia. I spent the latter part of the day exhausted, and frustrated. I felt imprisoned in my body; there was no way out. During the day, I watched the clock moving, so slowly, until it was time for me to start getting ready for bed. Then I could take my pill and sleep.

Some of the things I couldn't do: lift a tea kettle, open the refrigerator door with one hand, blow-dry my hair, carry a tall glass of water, or do anything heavy—drive a car, do laundry, go food shopping, or empty the dishwasher. I used hand towels after a shower. I couldn't lift a full bath towel. Getting things done took a lot of time. One day I wrote out a check and mailed it. It took all day because of the strain on my back to reach for my checkbook, the strain on my shoulders and upper back as I wrote the check, the strain to reach for the stamps, and the very slow walk to the mailbox.

David did all the chores. When I couldn't drive the car, he often drove me to physical therapy. He would wait in the car for me, reading *The New York Times*, as if there were nowhere else he needed or wanted to be.

While the pain from the muscle spasms prevented me from doing things, I got all sorts of help from friends and family. When I needed to get a few extra things from the supermarket, a friend of mine came with me, because I couldn't handle lifting any packages. I'd point things out, and Barbara would put them in the cart for me. Then she piled everything in her car, drove me home and brought the groceries in.

Martha helped me with my winter clothes. I had told her that I was afraid moths would wreak havoc with my wool things. I didn't mean to be manipulative when I said it. I was surprised when she offered to help. She put some bags of my clothes in a shopping cart, took them to the dry cleaners, and lifted them out and put them on the counter. I couldn't have done that.

Megan arrived from Manhattan, and helped me in the supermarket to get a few things. I was wearing black braces on both wrists for the tendonitis, and I could barely handle the packages. "Mom, let me do it. You look like The Claw." She was relieved that I found that funny. At home, she did my laundry and hung up the clothes that had been piling up on the floor. She did other things that I wasn't capable of, like bringing up the fan from the basement, things like that.

One afternoon the pain and frustration made me cry—silently. I was afraid to sob, because it might set off a spasm. I cried and knew it was useless, that it wouldn't change anything, that I wouldn't feel better for it. Sometimes I would say to Dave, "I'm hurting," when it got particularly bad. That didn't make me feel better either. I was exhausted in the afternoons because I wasn't able to sleep. No matter how hard I tried, no matter where I positioned pillows, it was impossible. Maybe all the pain and frustration contributed to this next episode. Maybe leaving the Church contributed too. Maybe it was just the "right time."

Unlike prior episodes, I had physical symptoms. In the beginning my whole body shook. I lost my appetite. My cousin Patricia advised yogurt; even frozen yogurt would do, she said. David walked me down to the local ice cream shop and I had vanilla frozen yogurt in a cup, but I didn't finish it.

It was a while before I began to eat normally. One morning I prepared breakfast, and sprinkled some raisins on my cereal. The raisins scared me. I was afraid I was going to hallucinate. I quickly put the cereal away.

Hallucinations plagued me during this episode. Hallucinations terrify me more than anything else. I have even less control over them than I do over my thoughts. I can fight for my thoughts, but what can I do about the hallucinations? I can tell myself that they're not real, and I do tell myself that, but that doesn't make them go away. One night, I woke up to the sound of David saying something to me. Even while I was hearing him talk to me, I knew that I was hallucinating. He wasn't saying anything at all.

The auditory hallucinations were full-blown delusions, compared to the visual ones. Many times I'd be just on the brink of hallucinating visually, then it would recede. I'd look at the ties on a lounge chair, for example, and see them about to morph into snakes. But that's as far as it would get. The snakes would only threaten to appear. My tactile sense also felt the brunt of the hallucinations. I felt snakes winding their way around my ankles, but mercifully it didn't last long.

As usual, I had strange thoughts. As I walked up the street in my town one day, there happened to be fewer and fewer people about. I thought that the reason that there were fewer people was because the people I could see weren't real people, just manifestations of my perceptions. None of them was a real person. Seeing fewer people was a sign that I was growing in my enlightenment, because it meant that I was seeing fewer "fake" people. I realized that, in fact, there were no other people, just David and me. We were Adam and Eve, and this was the Garden of Eden. The more I came to realize this, the more the beauty and joy of the Garden would become evident.

The hallucinations eventually stopped, and so did most of the strange thoughts, but I was still not quite recovered, and not quite ready to be by myself. Before the episode, I had made appointments to see three doctors in the city in one day. The appointments had been made in a burst of efficiency, when I had been feeling my usual self. I was anxious to keep the appointments, but now there was no way that I could go alone to even one of them. My cousin Patricia told me "I'll be there, Eileen." She came in from Long Island, and met me in Manhattan. We made each appointment, and she waited for me while I was being seen. We had lunch at the cafeteria of a hospital. Despite the circumstances of my illness, we managed to talk nonstop, exchanging our customary understanding looks and smiles, and laughing together, as we always did.

When I had fully recovered mentally, I went to play bridge with the seniors. I thought that that would take my mind off my physical troubles. Instead, I found that handling the cards hurt too much, and I decided to leave. One of the women called me over. "You sit here next to me," she said. She told me to look at her cards and tell her which card I wanted to play. Then she played that card for me. I came home and told David about what one of "my women" had done.

I wonder about the theory that we always have everything we need. I think about political prisoners being tortured, for example. Surely, they don't have everything they need. I think about refugees, and victims of violent crimes. It doesn't seem as though they have everything they need. Yet in my personal experience, it seems like I *have* had everything I needed. When things have been bleak, I *have* been buoyed up. So I often wonder about it.

I have to really learn that inside (each) self
is the Spirit, the Buddha.

Chapter 24

Prelude

Euphoria, psychosis, depression. That's the usual pattern. The euphoria is a smooth and seductive path that lets me see life as radiant, awash in a golden glow. Odd that the prelude to such misery should be so much fun.

In this ecstatic state, I understand sacred teachings, including the parables of Jesus Christ, Zen stories, and mystical basics, such as that we are all one. I live in a world of possibilities. I know that the human race is only one step away from lasting peace. We are alive in a luminescent world. I feel intensely spiritual. I understand many sacred things that ordinarily would remain a mystery to me. I'm in tune with the energies of the universe. Only good can happen in this world; it's a little like heaven. My different thoughts about the nature of existence fit together to make an elegant whole.

I have unbelievable bouts of energy. There's no task too daunting for me to accomplish. I'm wired. I get by with much less sleep. I delight in spending large sums of money without a second thought. Everything I do is effortless. I feel buoyant, and optimistic about my life. I feel capable of doing anything I want. I can sing. I can move like a dancer. I can write. I can even write poetry. I can interpret the poetry of others. I can stay up late. I can clean out my closet.

In this glorious world of euphoria, an invisible but tactile force surrounds me, a loving force. A beautiful energy guides my life, takes care of me. I live within that force, and nothing bad can touch me.

Thoughts start to race, but I keep up with them, delighted at how one thought bumps up against another, and another. Later on, thoughts will come to me so fast that I won't be able to keep track of them. It will feel as if they're attacking me. I'll fly from one half-formed thought to another. Until then, I marvel at my thoughts, the secrets they reveal to me, their beauty.

Then, inevitably, comes the crash. I am in hell; I fight demons; I am menaced and terrorized; I am traumatized; I am in the nightmare; I see things that aren't really there and I can't make them go away; I struggle to discern the truth with an untrustworthy tool—my mind; I am prey for a malevolent force. When that part is over, it's time for depression, usually six months of meaninglessness and exhaustion.

When it's all over, I wonder whether the loving force that I experienced could really exist. If it did, could it exist, not just in my extraordinary life, but in ordinary life as well? Could there really be a hell, led by a calculating, intelligent, evil force that intends to possess me? Or do both forces exist, one loving, one evil? Or is there nothing at all?

Things make sense or they don't.

Chapter 25

The Doctor

As for personal information about him, I have gleaned only this much. I surmise that he is, or has been, married. I guess by the way he nods his head when we talk of children, that he has some of his own. I suspected, as I stood on the street outside his door (I was early) and saw him rounding the corner, that he lives in Manhattan. He looked so completely at home as he walked along, and living in the city would suit him—its culture, its variety, its intelligence and energy. But I'm not all that sure that he lives there. It's only a guess. Oh, yes, and his computer is a Macintosh. I know that.

He has a beautiful Persian rug in his office that has been there for at least as long as I have. The colors of his office are gray, black, honey-colored wood and the red of the carpet. He sometimes gets a cold, but is otherwise extraordinarily healthy. He has books and more books, and likes the air in his office cool.

Professionally, getting to know him well enough to trust him took a while. Learning to trust another person always does. Besides, at the beginning, I wasn't sane enough to trust anybody. I needed Angelo to be with me just to set foot in his office. Then I got a little bit saner and could be in his office by myself, but I couldn't stay still for the whole session. Whenever I got scared enough, I would leave his office to get a drink of water. After that happened a few times, he asked me if I was really thirsty or if I was frightened. I admitted to being frightened and wanting to get away. He asked me to stay, even when I got frightened. I tried it. It was a little bit scary, but I found I could do it. Now I stay put, like a normal person.

Most times I just walk into his office at a regular pace; but when things are shaky, I rush into the room like a frightened bird looking for sanctuary. I breathe in the familiar atmosphere—the smell of rug and furniture and books. I look at the furnishings, the prints on the walls, the glass table with the tissue box on it next to my chair, the desk with so many papers on it, the gray couch that I've never been on, his black leather chair and the footrest he sometimes uses, the air conditioner that he usually lowers when I come in. In just a few seconds, I take it all in. I look at him, so familiar, so distant, so close.

I know he can help me sort out what's real. I don't substitute his opinion for mine, but his opinion means a great deal. His face is expressive, whether he's thoughtful, or concerned, or sympathetic, or at times smiling. Sometimes he laughs. I bring him my issues in a tangled knot. He pulls a thread here, another one there. He asks me, "Do you think . . . Do you feel . . . Could it be . . . Have you ever thought that . . . Why do . . . Did your feeling that way have anything to do with . . . " He loosens the knot; I am better off than when I started.

I've brought him many issues. Sometimes, I bring in one issue and it turns out to be something else. He knows enough about my family to write its history. I talk about the conclusions I've drawn from my experiences. Some of them are right on the mark, some of them are distorted. I tell him things I would be afraid to tell anyone else. I learn things, about myself— who am I really, how do I sabotage myself, how do I support myself, when am I brave, and when do I avoid the truth? I learn about how to forgive my parents. And that it's the only way to get past the damage.

Forgiving my mother was easier, because I understood her defenses, and what she was defending against. Understanding her is, and always has been, instinctive, even before I suffered the same way she did. Even before I was afraid, as she was, of it happening again. It was easy for me to grasp the full significance of "Don't upset your father."

For a woman with her talents, living in the straightjacket of the 1950s, it's easy to see why she shied away from devoting herself to being our mother. She didn't want to be just a housewife, or somebody's mother, or somebody's wife. She needed her own identity, and only subliminally recognized the forces marshaled against her. She loved as she could. Whether that was the best she could do is not for me to know, though I tend to think it was.

Forgiving my father took longer. His lack of self-esteem was hard to forgive, his self-pity, his bias against women. His attitude that women were useless unless they were pretty—that was hard to forgive. He was contradictory. On the one hand, he encouraged and praised my talents—in later years he would be proud of my being a lawyer; on the other, he placed enormous importance on how I looked, and whether I dressed well. I know he had his own demons to fight, demons that shaped him into the way he was. I know that he hadn't had the best of childhoods. I know he had to fight his past. I just didn't care for his weapons.

He tended to feel sorry for himself. He was telling my mother his troubles one time, about his difficult boss, about whether he had enough money for three kids who were getting ready for college, about everyday things. Finally he said, "Well, Christ said, 'Carry your cross,' and I guess that's what I have to do."

My mother, who had not said a word while he recited his troubles, then said, "Christ said 'carry' your cross, not 'drag' it." He laughed at her unexpected and fitting response, but it didn't stop him from going back to his old habit of bemoaning his life.

He was never satisfied with who he was, how far he had come in his career, with his life. There was only some evidence that he was grateful for his blessings or grateful for being the man he was. It was hard to forgive his negativity.

But I learned to replace anger with pity. I replaced some of the pity with admiration. We don't all start the race on the same starting line. Everybody starts from their own place. Where you finish is relative to where you started out.

I don't forgive my parents because I owe it to them; I forgive them because it's good for me. It's my way to erase the unwitting wounding that they each did. To some extent, forgiving is possible because of understanding. To some extent, it's possible because their hurtful attitudes were merely expressions of their own issues. They were not personal to me. Nothing hurtful ever is. So I regret what might have been, and am thankful for what was. Thankful to my mother, for example, for her immersion in a spiritual life; thankful to my father for his ethics, for wanting to be a good man.

It's hardest to forgive myself—for all the wrong choices in my life, for not valuing myself, for not realizing that I am as worthwhile as the next person even though I may not be as talented, for being naive, for being intimidated by anyone or anything, for expecting too much from myself, for expecting too little, for having great instincts but not acting on them, for being fragile, worried, easily upset, high-strung, for blaming myself for periodically going insane, for striving for perfection, for striving at all, for working too hard, for feeling obligated to do what other people want, for seeking approval, for forgetting that the Spirit lives within me and that it keeps me safe, for being judgmental, for self-criticism that goes too far, for looking to the wrong people to be a mirror for myself. Forgiving myself is the most difficult. I'm still working on it.

Recently Dr. Schein said to me, "We've worked together for a lot of years." "*We've* worked." He wasn't taking all the credit for my deepened understanding and awareness. "We."

It's true that we have worked together a long time. I've known him through many incarnations of myself. Known him when I was just coming out of my hippie stage. I'd been to Woodstock. I believed in peace on earth, loving my brother and sister, smoking pot. I wore beads that a friend of mine had strung together for me. She also made her own candles, using cut-down cardboard milk cartons to form the shapes. I thought that was the most creative thing I'd ever seen. She'd also lived on a commune, something I would never do. It sounded great in theory, but it also sounded like a lot of dirt and hard physical work.

My next incarnation was as a corporate attorney, complete with briefcase, commute, meetings, a "B" office (more windows) and a speakerphone (a status symbol before they decided to give one to everybody).

Then marriage and all the ins and outs of making that work.

Motherhood, my most fulfilling experience. I had been brought up on the feminist movement and believed that having children meant wiping snotty noses and enduring hours of dullness and drudgery. I was so surprised to find out how wrong that view was. To find out how much fun it could be to relate to a living, loving creature. To embrace, to do projects together, to talk, to listen.

Now I'm in a new phase. Marriage is steady, I no longer raise my child—she's an adult now—and there is no job. I explore life and myself, feeling more confident than I ever did when I had the trappings of success.

I like to mix and match ideas about the nature of existence, some from physics, some from religion, some from beyond even science and religion. I learned recently that every mass has stored in it a tremendous amount of energy. Maybe feeling energy, not only from people, but from inanimate objects, isn't so esoteric after all.

So I've been through all these stages and more with Dr. Schein. He provides a very wide context. He doesn't think me crazy for having a far-out idea, just so long as I'm balanced. It is easier to get well and to stay healthy when I don't have to censor myself. I could say he's nonjudgmental, but he does judge when I'm going too far afield—when my ideas are colliding, going too fast, and being a harbinger of bad times to come. Not to mention judging when my ideas are really crazy. Ordinarily, he doesn't argue with my vision of reality, but when I'm getting too manic, then that's another story.

I called him one time when I was falling into a bad state, just teetering on the edge. "I'm not doing so well," I tell him. "I can hear that," he says. When I'm not well, he tells me to call him between visits to check in. I do. He listens, talks to me, asks a few questions, advises me about my medication, and ends with "And call me anytime." Sometimes I take him up on it.

One night, before I dropped off to sleep, I got to thinking about philosophy, theology, and the nature of things. I got an insight; it was a mystical moment. *Or else I'm manic*, I thought. I decided not to take any chances; when I next saw him I told him about it.

The temptation is to not tell him about things that could be manic, so that he won't think I'm starting to crash. And if he doesn't think I'm starting to crash, then I'm most probably not. I know that telling him or not telling him doesn't alter the facts. I know that, but it still takes some inner effort to admit to him that I might not be quite all right. If he should think so too, then the abyss is not far away.

So I told him about my insight. I was relieved when he said, "I don't think you were manic. I think you had a mystical moment." I was relieved that he had the scope to encompass mystical moments, because I love mine and want to have as many as possible in this lifetime. I don't want to have to deny them in order to be judged sane, or have to argue their legitimacy, or not feel comfortable expressing them for fear of a lack of understanding or downright disapproval.

Every year, I have to do without him while he goes on vacation. I always get a little anxious about it. By now, I expect to feel anxious as soon as he tells me his vacation dates, which he always gives well in advance. Since I've had a lot of practice with this, I can quiet myself somewhat just by knowing the source of my anxiety. I also know that I can call his answering machine when he's away. "Hello, this is Dr. Schein, speaking to you on a recording." I often wonder if anybody living in this century would really think that he wasn't speaking on a recording, but I let it pass. I just listen to his voice, and then hang up. I know that if that's not enough, I can always call the covering doctor whose information he always leaves on the machine.

He's not what I would call a Freudian, although he has a keen interest in dreams. I often bring him a dream that I've analyzed for myself already, only to find that he has a different take on it. I usually wind up agreeing with him that my analysis was letting me deny an issue, the same way my dream was camouflaging something, keeping its meaning from me.

We don't always agree on what's happening with me. When I disagree with his opinion, he doesn't push too hard, frequently not at all. Sometimes, I can tell that he accepts my outlook; other times I think maybe he's just being quiet.

I don't know much about him, but I know enough. He has intellect and humor, honesty and compassion. That's enough.

Even when you're innocent,
you get slammed.

Chapter 26

Intentions and Expectations

It will never happen again. It won't. I can feel it. Look at me now, handling my life, paying bills, organizing things, staying in touch with friends, loving my family, participating in my clubs, keeping my appointments, including all the doctors I have on my list, even going to my dentists on a regular schedule. I am so handling my life.

I am absolutely ordinary. Except for an undercurrent of anxiety, I function fine. I engage in intelligent conversation. I listen intently when people want my attention, puzzle out what they might need from me. I'm at least as mature and insightful as the next person. I'm so normal, just like everybody else. There's nothing wrong with me.

There really isn't—now. I can't fool myself though. That next atom bomb is going to explode soon. It's been three years since the last one. How much longer will I last? Another year? Two at the most?

Psychosis is a thief that steals not only my peace of mind, but also the ordinary give-and-take of my relationships. There's no give on my part, only take. I lean on my favorite people. I am needy. I scare my daughter and my husband. I frighten my friends, get everyone concerned.

Sometimes I get shaky moments, not atom-bomb moments, but just difficult ones. I try to hide them. I don't want to lean too heavily on the threads of my relationships. I don't want anyone to see me as not quite all there, as needing help or, God forbid, needing to be watched over.

Perversely, I challenge the next episode to arrive. I want to see how well I will maintain myself next time. Am I getting any better at it? Can I take in that influx of energy without getting overloaded? How much have I learned? Enough? Can I be in touch with its energy and its insights and not succumb to the lure of mania? Can I hold on to the good vibes I get, and avoid the feeling that I'm being pursued by the devil? And if I can't shake the feeling that I am being pursued by the devil, can I hold on to all that's good in the universe and know that the devil can't touch me if I hold on tight enough? Can I ride the crest of that energy, be in control of it, and not fall into the screaming heebie-jeebies? Actually, I'm not really a screamer. I'm more like the abused dog that shies away from an outstretched hand.

The wait for the next episode is, by turns, ominous and hopeful. On the hopeful side, I recently had an indirect encounter with a swan that left me feeling pretty good. I was strolling through the grounds of a park. There were geese and swans. I had never heard a swan call, and I expected it to be as melodious as a swan is graceful. Not so. It sounded more like a cross between a crow's caw and a goose's honk. This particular swan stood about two feet from a couple who had stopped to admire the geese and swans. It stretched out its neck and "cawnked" loudly at them. Several times. Was it angry? Did it want to shoo them away? Did it want them to feed it? Something was going on in the swan's head that it was trying to communicate.

I had never given the intelligence of swans any thought before, but I recognized this attempt to communicate as a sign of intelligence. Then I thought about dogs, and cats, and not-too-bright sheep, horses, and so many other animals. I thought of this one pool of intelligence in which all sensate beings dipped. I thought about how our intelligence all comes from the same source. How we are all connected through that pool.

If I were in a manic phase, I would have felt heavy vibrations in my head, like a huge gong being struck. I would have wondered about the swan. Was it talking to me, and just pretending to talk to this other couple? Was I supposed to know what it was saying? Was this the swan from the mythic story of Zeus, who had assumed the form of a swan and taken the woman, Leda, as his mate? Was I seeing Zeus? Was I seeing God? Were all the animals talking to me? Should I approach the swan, talking its language? Was I in Paradise?

None of those things occurred to me. It gives me hope that I can handle tiny bits of energy. Maybe I can handle increased amounts. Maybe I can.

Meanwhile, I await the next episode. While I'm waiting, I constantly take my mental temperature. How much stress am I under? How much can I do about it? Any nightmares lately? How are the panic attacks? More frequent? More violent? Are they blending together in one long frightening stream? What to do about the stress of the illness itself?

I worry. What will happen when my doctor retires? What will happen if I go to a hospital in an emergency, and it's days before I can get my meds? What will happen if David dies first and I have no one to give me advance warning when I need it, or to back me up, sober me, when I'm in the middle of it? What am I feeling now? Is it sadness or the beginnings of depression? Fear comes out of nowhere; I remind myself that that's where it belongs.

I know everyone has their sorrows. I know of a few sorrows that I wouldn't trade for mine. Still, I envy people. I envy people who aren't afraid of the day when their minds will betray them, again. I see a woman parking a car, or a man walking into a movie theater, or a couple coming out of a restaurant, or walking down the street with their kids, or a man running for the train, or a woman getting her nails done, or greeting a neighbor, stopping to talk. I envy them all. They remind me of the inhabitants of *Our Town*, these people who think nothing of the precious normalcy of their lives—the everyday sights and smells and loves and relationships. People who don't realize what normal is because they've never known anything else.

Sometimes, for no reason at all—I might be looking out at my backyard, or walking down the street, or breathing the summer air at dusk—I feel quiet and I know what normal is like. I know what I'd be like if I were free. Free. Normal. I would experience only the sort of strain inherent in daily living. The kind I experience already, in fact, but without the illness underneath. As it is, the strains of my life press on the existing strain of the illness itself, always the illness. I'm more fragile than I'd like to be.

Sometimes I imagine what my life would have been like without the illness. What other things would I have done? How much less tension would I have had, how much more energy? But this leads absolutely nowhere. When I start to sink into the wishful, useless longing of "wouldn't life be wonderful if I were normal," I remind myself of what I've learned through my experiences with madness. I remind myself of who I am, and could only be, because of all the experiences I've had in my life.

Love is the binding force.

Chapter 27

Things That Help Me

The episodes hit me with the energy of a lightning bolt. If I'm not grounded, they blow me away. I try frantically to stay grounded, which might explain why I crave junk food during an episode. I find myself desperate for soda and pizza, potato chips, and cheeseburgers on rolls with fries and onion rings. Old TV shows seem to help in that particular way also, like *Dragnet* or *Perry Mason*, and old black-and-white movies, too. In some of the old movies, there are venetian blinds making patterns against the wall. I especially love seeing the shadows the blinds make; I just love it. My brother Kevin once sent me videos of *The Adventures of Dr. Fu Manchu*. They were very relaxing. Maybe in part because bad is always thwarted; good triumphs. In the end, the world is safe.

Many people and things have helped me during the various stages of my illness. I am thankful for them all, and for the Spirit that inspired them. Depending on the stage I'm in, I might require different kinds of help.

During depression, some things that help me are:

Time (After enough time, the depression slowly, magically, and mercifully lifts.)

Sleep (Not a cure, certainly, but it helps me to live through it.)

Nonjudgmental attitudes from those I love

Medication

An excellent therapist

At the onset of psychosis, the thing that helps me is:

Experience—the preliminaries to an episode are less likely to trap me so easily now. I distrust that golden glow that invariably precedes an episode. I know that incredible beauty and energy can lead to horror, and I call my doctor. I see him more often than usual, and also get extra meds. Catching it early doesn't make it go away, but it lessens the intensity. Perhaps the duration as well.

During psychosis, some things that help me are:

An excellent therapist

Medication

Acceptance from those I love

A belief from those I love that I will be all right—even that somewhere inside, I am already all right

Caring from those I love—patience, conversations, phone calls, visits, help with practical things

Junk food

Old movies; old TV shows

My mantras—the mantras came about during an episode when I was struggling to tell what was real and what wasn't.

It would be hard to say which is the most important item on the list, but the one I use most often is definitely the mantras. They act as an aid for me to know what to believe. During an episode, I get so torn between conflicting ideas. Are people reading my mind or not? How can I know for sure? How can I trust anyone else to tell me? I can't trust myself to judge; I know by now that I'm unreliable. Is that seductive malevolent force right? Must I sink further into that fearful blackness? How can I know what's right when I know I can't trust myself?

During one of my episodes (third? fourth?), I got an insight that helped me. I had been wrestling with the problem of how to know what was true, and finally concluded that the dreadful thoughts couldn't be true. They were terrifying and horrifying and they led to a bad place. But that wasn't why they weren't true. The reason they weren't true was because they weren't loving. Love was reality, the only reality. I could cling to that.

It was a powerful idea: *Love is the only reality*. I judged everything by that standard. And later, another mantra came out of that one: *If it isn't loving, it isn't real.* Now, whenever psychotic thoughts threaten to pry loose my slender grip on reality, I repeat the mantras.

I use them to battle the familiar, psychotic thoughts. I know I've had these strange thoughts before. Knowing I've had these thoughts before, however, doesn't make me think that they're lies. Instead, my mixed-up mind believes that my past psychotic episodes have always been the true reality, and that the sanity I've enjoyed in between bouts only served to deceive me. I start to be seduced by such ideas as:

The person I'm talking to is in disguise.

People can read my mind.

I deserve the humiliation I'm feeling.

The devil is invading me.

The evil that I feel is real; I have to succumb to it.

I use one of my mantras as a litmus test. How can it be true that people can read my mind, when that's not loving? How can the devil invade my mind when love is the only reality? How can I succumb to fear when fear is not loving? The struggle to decide what is real is tremendous; it takes all my strength. The mantras help me choose what to believe.

After one of my episodes was over, I started to wonder how I could be so sure that love is the reality. What am I basing my belief on? I was surprised to realize that I'm not basing my belief on anything. It's a leap of faith, not a mathematical theorem, a belief and not a fact. I choose to believe that Love does underpin the universe. It enables every living thing to breathe. It is ever present, ever available.

The mantras are not a perfect shield against the insanity that assails me, but they have saved me from sinking into hell many, many times. They remind me that evil is always a lie. Love is what's real, the rest just smoke and mirrors.

Recently, I've acquired another mantra. It soothes me, and always gives me hope that I have not lost the sanctity of my own mind. The violation I always feel during an episode is just another evil lie. I am still, and always, myself. The mantra is:

Love is sanity, and it is real.

Living sane in an insane world—
the challenge and the goal.

Chapter 28

Another World

Demons, hallucinations, paranoia, and other pathways to hell are all a part of my psychotic state, but they're not the whole experience, especially not in my later episodes. Other things happen too. My intuitive powers soar, and I sense things that ordinarily I can't.

It would be more accurate to call those aspects of my episodes part of an altered state of consciousness, rather than a psychotic state. The experience isn't totally crazy; some of it just differs from normal life.

In an altered state, I can see energy. It radiates from people in translucent, gray, wavy lines. On subway platforms, and in other crowded places, I see the pathways of energy as people move about. Sometimes, I just accept the phenomenon as one of the signal traits of my state of mind. Other times, if I'm feeling vulnerable, seeing energy can frighten me because it means I'm near, or already in, another episode. I have no control over whether I'll see the energy or not. I think that someday I might be able to learn that control.

Seeing energy might just be a hallucination of sorts, but I don't believe that. We all have energy. Why couldn't seeing it be a developing sense that we'll all have sooner or later, as part of our natural state?

I feel the energy in plants and trees, too. I was in my backyard one difficult day, and for some reason, put my hand on the trunk of a small dogwood tree. Quite unexpectedly, I felt energy emanating from the tree, a healing, benevolent energy.

Energy from plants hasn't always felt friendly. One day as I was coming home, I could feel the energy coming from the shrubs as I came up the walk. It made the shrubs seem larger than they were, and I felt a looming intelligence in them. Even the front door was in emanation mode. *I really don't want to get into this right now,* I thought. Instantly, the world around me got more normal. When I told my doctor about it, he was pleased. Maybe I was developing a skill, he said, something to de-sensitize me.

During an episode, I know certain things that ordinarily I wouldn't. One time, I called my psychiatrist because I could feel myself being sucked into a bad state. I couldn't handle it by myself; I needed to see him. When he answered the phone, he said he would look in his book to find out whether he could see me that day. Well, that was silly. Of course he could see me that day. I felt his availability in the quality of the air pressing around me in my living room, and in the air between us on the phone. I could feel it as tangibly as the brush of a cat's tail along my arm. It was a different kind of knowing, that's all.

I had more than the quality of the air around me as a guide to knowing that he'd see me. I also had a conviction that my need would be met. I didn't just *want* to see him, or think it would be nice or helpful. I *needed* to see him, and the universe would arrange it so that I was able to. (Didn't he know that?) The conviction that my need would be met was not only a belief, but a tangible feeling, like feeling the ripples in a pool from a stone dropped into the water. Subtle, but tactile. Whenever I've bottomed out in an episode, the universe has come through for me. I knew it would at that particular moment.

Yes, I saw him that day.

I know when things are going to happen before they do. I can tell when the phone is about to ring, or when music on the radio will turn soothing, or when someone will show up on the doorstep, or when David will suggest something relaxing, like a walk, or dinner out. (If I'm too shaky, it's dinner at the diner, rather than a formal restaurant, and if I'm really shaky then we don't go out at all.)

Usually, I get these precognitive moments when I'm having a particularly hard time. It starts with the quality of the air. In an altered state, the air is thicker, like honey. At the same time, the air is thin and breathable, much like in dreams where contradictory things constantly coexist. I feel something in the heavy air pressing against my arms, and I know that someone/something is coming to help me.

I liken my heightened sensitivity to the way a spider's web works. A drop of rain on a strand of a spider's web sets off vibrations that can be felt throughout the web. When the loving gesture of a friend reaches out to help me, it's like that drop of rain on a strand of that web. It lets me feel my friend's energy flowing toward me.

After an episode is over, I think about those moments of precognition; they seem much too unusual, miraculous even. They're not to be believed. But I do believe them. They were real. Energies travel, and the universe works to take care of us whenever possible. Physics will explain it all adequately someday.

But if the universe is so caring, why do I suffer at all? I've come to terms with that question (somewhat) through the fairy tale of Sleeping Beauty. In that story, the evil witch puts a curse on the young princess—she will die at age sixteen. Only one good witch remains to bestow a favor on the child. She says that she doesn't have the power to undo the curse, but she can lessen it by having the princess sleep one hundred years instead of dying. I think of good and evil that way. What I suffer is evil, but there are cushions to help me along the way. I think a lot about good and evil, light and darkness. I think about how good and light have to win in the end. But for now, the war continues, and I, along with everyone else, am the battleground.

Despite the suffering, I've learned things that I wouldn't know so palpably if I had not been bipolar. The episodes aren't all lies. Ordinary life does encapsulate the extraordinary; there is Spirit within tangible things; Spirit may be tangible too, who knows. We really are all connected—our energies do touch upon one another.

In my backyard once, a robin came incredibly close to me. I didn't move. It came close enough that I could almost touch it. It made me think about the quality of being still. Of being quiet enough so that things would come to me. Like Saint Francis and the animals, like monks and awareness.

On a summer day in the middle of an episode, I was walking up the block, wishing I had someone with me to help me. I was suffering physically, and mentally I was just hanging on. It was a beautiful day, a cloudless sky, the flowers were out, a bird was calling, the grass was a vivid green, with each blade doing its part to make the whole. The energy of life was vibrant in each and every living thing, right down to the individual blades of grass. I felt that the very cells in all the life around me contained a pathway for a healing energy, an energy that was powerful, wholesome, and kind. Access to this energy did not depend on a phone call, or a friendly visit, or music, or anything. It was within every living thing, inextricably present, always accessible to me. Still to learn: It is always within myself.

My goal is to have an episode without the delusions, the paranoia, the shaky vulnerability. Instead, just an altered state of consciousness, in which I'll have paranormal gifts that won't freak me out. That's the goal, anyway. I would rather not have the episodes that inevitably will come, but if I have to have them, couldn't I transmute them into a more useful form? That's the hope, anyway.

It's a balancing act—between the demons on the one hand, and the visions on the other. What I need to do is to walk the tightrope of normal life, still realizing that I'm following an extraordinary path. To know that I've been blessed with having brushed up against the soul of God, and cursed with the chilly touch of a monster who came knocking on my door. To learn how to be a mystic without being a lunatic. To struggle less, and to laugh more often. To wrestle my delusions to the ground, once and for all. To have an ordinary life, even knowing what I know. To focus solely on that precious state of sanity, at once delicate and robust. To maintain my balance. To walk a fine line.

Acknowledgments

For helping to bring this book to life, I am deeply grateful to

Shobha Vanchiswar, who started it all by enrolling me in our writing workshop, and who gave me her unflagging support right from the beginning.

Joan Schulman, who taught my writing workshop with discernment and skill.

Elyse Locurto, who spent hours deftly editing my work with insight, flair and perseverance.

Heidi Hellmich, who reviewed the manuscript and gave me many valuable suggestions.

Everyone who read and commented on the manuscript.

I could not have managed without their concern, encouragement, and enthusiasm.

For supporting me in my life, I am deeply grateful to

My brothers, and my cousins, who pray for me, who make me laugh, and who are always on my side.

Dr. Jonah Schein, who helps make the terrifying times less frightening, the bad times better, and the good times more enhanced.

David, for his incredible patience, love, and support.

Megan, for her laughter, understanding, and love. For herself.